ANGLIA EAST

The first locomotive-hauled passenger train to reach Norwich was a BR staff special which ran on 9 April 1987 hauled by 86 246. It is seen here on the return trip crossing the new Trowse Swing Bridge. The overhead contact wire can be seen feeding into a fixed rail above the cab of the locomotive. (Another overhead rail, staggered to the right, carries current over the swinging section of the bridge which starts at the third portal)

THE TRANSFORMATION OF A RAILWAY

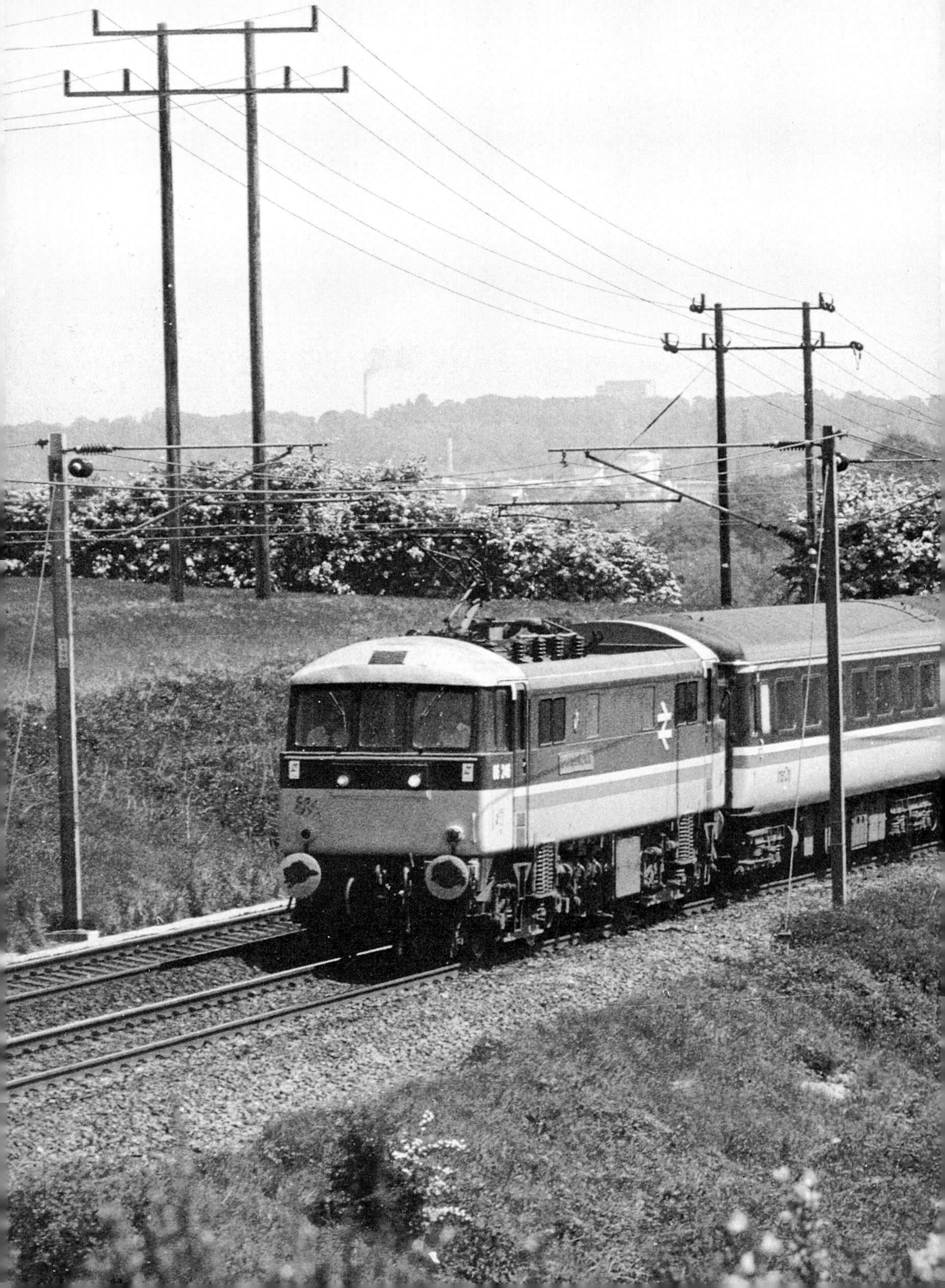

IAN COWLEY

ANGLIA EAST

DAVID & CHARLES

Newton Abbot   London
North Pomfret (Vt)

In happy memory of Doris

Contents

All photographs are by the author unless otherwise stated

British Library Cataloguing in Publication Data

Cowley, Ian
  Anglia East : the transformation of a
  railway.
  1. British Rail. *Eastern Region* ——
  History 2. Railways —— England —— East
  Anglia —— History —— 20th century
  I. Title
  385'.09426   HE3019.E2

  ISBN 0-7153-8978-5

Typeset by P&M Typesetting Ltd, Exeter
and printed in Great Britain
by Redwood Burn Limited, Trowbridge, Wilts
for David & Charles Publishers plc
Brunel House Newton Abbot Devon

Published in the United States of America
by David & Charles Inc
North Pomfret Vermont 05053 USA

Class 309 units 601 and 622 formed the first electric train to Norwich on 6 April 1987 when they tested overhead line equipment. The pair are seen departing from Thorpe station virtually hidden by catenary. Compare this picture to those on page 36.

Introduction

East Anglians certainly cannot claim that electrification took them by surprise, since the possibility was first raised in the Modernisation Plan of 1955. On second thoughts, that the plans finally became reality may have been something of a shock to people who had heard it all several times before!

Once electrification with its attendant track rationalisation and resignalling becomes a reality, the face of the railway is irrevocably changed and one theme of this book is to show these changes by way of illustrations.

To have electrified from London to Norwich and Harwich from scratch would never have been approved in the 1980s, so the Anglia projects owe their existence to the foundations laid by preceding schemes which came to fruition during a period when the railways faced a somewhat more favourable political and economic climate. The second theme of this book is an examination of developments in the GE area prior to Anglia East.

A word of clarification: throughout the book, I refer to 'the GE area'. By this I mean all the surviving lines of the old Great Eastern Railway together with the former London Tilbury & Southend Railway lines, control of which passed to the Eastern Region in 1949. Also in the interests of brevity, locomotive and multiple unit types are generally referred to by their current TOPS classifications.

This book could not have been written without assistance generously given by many railwaymen, both professional and amateur. I gratefully acknowledge my especial debts to Peter Abbott, Alistair Barham, Ernst Birschler, Mike Collins, John Day, Graham Hardinge, Chris Hurricks, Harry James, Brian Leighton, Andy Lickfold, Mike Mallory, Cliff Wrate, John Yelverton and the Ipswich Transport Society. Finally, I am grateful to my wife, without whose encouragement this book would still be a heap of papers on the sitting room floor!

1 · Anglia East – the Background

Early Schemes

The Great Eastern Railway went to extreme lengths in the first 20 years of the century to avoid electrification. It is therefore more than a little ironic to find its main line to Norwich becoming only the second main (as opposed to suburban) line emanating from London north of the Thames to enjoy the benefit of the catenary.

The burgeoning growth of East London suburbia at the turn of the century saw several schemes aimed at tapping the traffic thus generated. Hoping to strengthen their case, the promoters sang the praises of the electrification which they proposed to adopt. To counter the threat to its territorial integrity, the GER went so far as to order A. J. Hill to design and build the unique 'Decapod' 0-10-0T,

Great Eastern development – 1: *A Liverpool Street–Cromer express headed by GE Claud Hamilton 4–4–0 No 1852 at Brentwood in the early years of the present century. While the front and back parts of the train comprise non-gangwayed coaches, in the centre is a three-coach corridor restaurant car set. (L&GRP)*

with the object of demonstrating that the touted capacity of electric traction to accelerate 300 odd tons to 30mph within 30 seconds could be matched by steam. By all accounts this is exactly what the extraordinary machine did, although only under test conditions and never in revenue-earning service. Having successfully seen off the threat of competition, the 'Decapod' was promptly rebuilt in the form of a rather ungainly 0-8-0 tender locomotive for freight work.

However, the growth in suburban traffic somewhat embarrassingly refused to abate – embarrassing because much of it was at concessionary rates which failed to generate sufficient revenue to justify expensive capital investment in electrification. Thus it was that after World War I the American Henry Thornton and his able lieutenant F. V. Russell set about the creation of the most intensive steam operated suburban service in the world – the famous 'Jazz trains'. Their introduction was prefaced by alterations to track layout and signalling, said to involve less than a

quarter the cost of electrification, before Holden's diminutive 0-6-0 and 0-4-4 tanks were unleashed on peak hour services which required 16-coach trains of four-wheelers to work at 2½-minute headways up Bethnal Green bank, and for turn-round times of just four minutes per train in the terminus. This enabled an increase of 50 per cent in the down evening rush hour service and of 75 per cent in the number of up morning peak hour trains to be achieved. During the peak hour 20,350 seats were available, greater, it was claimed, than any electric service in the country had provided up to that time. Punctuality records which would bring a gleam to the eye of today's Network SouthEast supremo Chris Green were achieved in the early years of this remarkable operation, but this was perhaps the Great Eastern's swan song as the railway lost its separate identity in the Grouping of 1923.

Its successor company, the London & North Eastern Railway, seemed less opposed to the principle of electrification; indeed, one of its first actions was to institute a feasibility study of electrification for the Great Eastern and Great Northern suburban services, but again financial constraints proved decisive.

The North and North East London Traffic Enquiry of 1925 added another voice to the clamour for improvement, but its echoing of a 1905 Royal

Great Eastern development – 2: *Fifty years on, and LNER Class B17 4–6–0 No 61601 Holkham starts the climb of Brentwood bank with a Liverpool Street–Clacton express in 1951. The original double track was widened to four tracks during the 1930s and in 1949 suburban services to Shenfield had been electrified. One of the electric trains stands in the reversing siding waiting to work its next trip back to Liverpool Street* (C. R. L. Coles)

Commission's recommendations for electrification proved no more fruitful. The finance impasse was not to be overcome until in 1935 the Government sanctioned the Treasury to guarantee interest on loans for capital work in order to relieve un-employment. The LNER took advantage of this in the London area with proposals to electrify the lines to Shenfield and Hackney Downs, and by agreement with the London Passenger Transport Board for the latter to extend its Central Line eastward from Liverpool Street, taking over the Loughton line of the old GER.

Electrification at 1,500V dc from Liverpool Street and Fenchurch Street to Shenfield was duly sanctioned.

World War II drastically delayed completion of the scheme, and it was to be under British Railways auspices that the electric service between Liverpool Street and Shenfield commenced in September 1949. The success of the new services may be

Great Eastern development – 3: *From 1951 new BR Standard Britannia class Pacifics took over a new interval timetable on Liverpool Street – Norwich services. Here No 70009* Alfred the Great *arrives at Liverpool Street on a hot August Saturday in 1960.* (M. C. Kemp)

judged by the decision to extend electrification to Chelmsford and Southend, implementing expansion which had been envisaged in 1935. Work on both lines was completed by the end of 1956.

In the meantime had come the quantum leap of the 1955 Modernisation Plan. To the various suburban electrification schemes under consideration at the time and which it recommended for adoption were to be added main line projects. The Plan recognised that the capacity to electrify was limited in the 15-year period with which it was concerned, and so it recommended work on two trunk routes: King's Cross–Doncaster, Leeds and (possibly) York, and Euston–Birmingham, Liverpool and Manchester, and on one with lesser traffic density.

in East Anglia the 'principal lines beyond Ipswich, and Bishop's Stortford'.

A re-appraisal of the Modernisation Plan in a White Paper (Cmd.893) of July 1959 deferred electrification beyond Colchester and on the GN main line until after 1964, although it recommended that the Bishop's Stortford–Cambridge extension should be implemented as partial compensation. Spiralling operating deficits led not only to the abandonment of such positive investment, but ushered in the traumatic reappraisal of the whole railway system in the Beeching years from 1962. Apart from the extension of the LMR scheme from Weaver Junction to Glasgow in May 1974 the story of main line electrification ceased for 20 years.

Suburban schemes

This, however, was not the case with less grandiose schemes on the suburban front, and the GE area of the Eastern Region continued to attract fairly constant investment. Following the Chelmsford and Southend extensions of the Shenfield scheme on the then standard BR system of 1,500V dc, the branch from Colchester–Clacton and Walton was selected for pilot work on the 25kV ac system, newly adopted for all but the SR in November 1955. Electric services on the Clacton line started in March 1959 and their success was confirmed by the conversion of the Southend branch to ac power (operating at 6.25kV) in November 1960. This coincided with the electrification of services between Liverpool Street and Enfield, Chingford, Hertford East and Bishop's Stortford, to be followed four months later by the conversion of Shenfield–Chelmsford to ac operation. Alternating current, mostly at 25kV, was now the new standard. June 1962 saw the closing of the gap between Chelmsford and Colchester, permitting through electric operation from Clacton and Walton. At the same time electric services commenced on the erstwhile London, Tilbury & Southend Railway lines from Fenchurch Street to Shoeburyness, administration of which had passed to the Eastern Region in 1949. In the London area of the GE little more remained to be done. May 1969 saw electrification extended up the Lea Valley from Clapton–Chestnut, before the reviving fortunes of the Braintree–Witham branch saw the catenary extended along the single track line in October 1977, bringing the total route mileage electrified in the GE area (including the LTS lines) to 233.

Main line plans

Despite the decision to concentrate main line electrification on the West Coast route, the Eastern Region electrification planning team was kept in

This third scheme envisaged the wires being extended beyond Chelmsford (to which town work was already in hand) to Ipswich, and included the branches to Clacton, Harwich and Felixstowe.

In the event, the British Transport Commission opted for action on the London Midland scheme, which it felt had greater passenger potential. However, that the other two schemes were at that stage postponed rather than abandoned is confirmed by the report of an Electrification Committee, charged with ironing out bottlenecks and allocating priorities in a rolling programme of electrification through to 1990. Following its first report in 1957, the BTC agreed to additional electrification in the period 1963-90 which included

The type that started it all. Preserved Class 306 unit No 017 is seen at Gidea Park on 15 November 1986. These units worked the pioneer GE electrification from Liverpool Street to Shenfield opened in 1949 and operating on the 1500V dc system. Depite a service life of more than thirty years, the class did not survive to see the completion of the Anglia schemes.

being, and although the Stedeford Committee had even questioned the viability of the LMR scheme the ER men continued their examination and appraisal of plans to extend the catenary along their own main lines.

Extension of GE electrification from Chelmsford to Ipswich, Harwich and Felixstowe was appraised in 1964/5 for both passenger and freight traffic. Freight from the LMR would have worked over the cross-London link provided by an ac electrified North London line to Gospel Oak and then via the Tottenham & Hampstead route to Forest Gate Junction en route to Barking and Tilbury. There being no link at Forest Gate to the GE main line in the down direction, it was also proposed to electrify from Tottenham (Copper Mill Junction) to Stratford, including part of Temple Mills Yard, to permit direct electric freight haulage from the LMR to the GE.

Poor financial returns and competing demands on limited resources saw the scheme consigned to the pending tray. The high cost of track and signalling work required to provide an immunised system pushed up the cost side of the calculation, the more so since some of the work would have been premature renewal. Freightliner traffic did not begin until 1965, while the boost to the revenue figures from the burgeoning growth of Felixstowe

as a container port could hardly have been foreseen.

The plans were dusted off in the early 1970s, by which time Freightliner growth had been insufficient to offset the general decline in freight traffic so that the cross-London link was abandoned and the proposal relied upon passenger traffic with freight haulage limited to spare time in the locomotives' passenger diagrams. Electrification of passenger services to Ipswich and Harwich was considered, involving push-pull working between London and Norwich. To minimise the time taken in changing locomotives at Ipswich, the northbound trains would be split, with diesel haulage of the front five coaches only, enabling high speed to be achieved to Norwich. The diesel would push its train back from Norwich to Ipswich to join up with the front portion of three or four coaches which would be waiting with its electric locomotive attached. The high cost of driving trailers ruled against this proposal and caused the planners to consider electrification right through to Norwich.

But by then the tide was beginning to turn, nationally and locally, in favour of the frustrated ER planners. At the national level, the first oil crisis of 1973 had not only intensified consciousness of energy conservation but had contributed to a seemingly remorseless rise in unemployment. In November 1977, following the recommendations of a Select Committee on Nationalised Industries, the Government announced its intention 'to review with the BRB the general case for further main line electrification on the basis of the up-to-date appreciation which it expects to receive shortly from

With the electrification of the first GE main line service between Liverpool Street and Clacton/Walton in the early 1960s high voltage alternating current was used from the start on much of the route although reduced voltage was employed at first on the inner suburban lines with automatic voltage changeover near Ingatestone. Here an inbound Clacton service passes Stratford for Liverpool Street in the late 1960s. (G. M. Kichenside)

Although Liverpool Street – Shenfield services were electrified in 1949 using the 1500V dc overhead system, by the early 1960s high voltage alternating current had become the new BR standard and in order not to inhibit future GE area electrification the original 1500V dc lines were converted initially to 6250V ac and later to 25,000V ac, entailing modification of the original Shenfield sets. Here one of the modified Shenfield sets waits at Seven Kings on a working to Gidea Park in July 1980. (M. L. Rogers)

the Board'. This was duly forthcoming in May 1978 in the form of a discussion paper entitled *Railway Electrification*. This showed traction costs per train mile as £0.80 for electric operation compared with £1.82 for diesel. Even when the capital and maintenance charges of the fixed capital required for electrification were considered, there remained an advantage of £0.56 per train mile for electric working.

At the local level much of the GE signalling north of Colchester was 70 or more years old and in need of renewal so that, coupled with judicious track rationalisation, the work would be self-financing due to the reduction in costs consequent upon replacing mechanical frame by power signalling, the closure of many manual boxes, and by economising on expensive track and point work. It might be thought that if track rationalisation and re-signalling paid for itself in terms of cost reduction, it would not harm the case for electrification to include such work in a single package. However, the discounted cash flow method of investment appraisal used by the Department of Transport to assess the viability of projects requiring its authorisation works on the basis that £1.00 now is worth more than £1.00 in the future. This is not because of inflation, but because of what the money might be earning elsewhere. The future costs and revenues of an investment project are therefore discounted and expressed in terms of their present value. The further into the future these money flows occur, the less will be their present value. Thus the high first costs of electrification are not greatly reduced by discounting because they occur right at the start of the project, whereas the revenue benefits are spread over the 30 years required by the exercise and are thus significantly reduced by the seven per cent test discount rate used. By being able to provide separate financial justification for the track and signalling work, their high initial cost could be taken out of the electrification calculations and thus raise the discounted rate of return on the latter project.

The scheme for resignalling and track rationalisation was duly submitted and approved in 1978, closely followed by comprehensive electrification proposals for Anglia West (Bishop's Stortford/Royston–Cambridge) and Anglia East (Colchester–Harwich/Norwich) submitted to the Department of Transport at the end of 1980.

By the early 1960s the Great Eastern area was largely dieselised apart from electric routes. However, Harwich and Norwich services ran with diesel traction under the electric catenary for much of their journeys. Main diesel types employed were Class 40s, 47s, 31s and 37s on passenger services. Here No 37 103 passes Ilford with the 09.40 Liverpool Street – Harwich Day Continental on 25 June 1980. (M. L. Rogers)

The Eastern Region recommended that work should commence on Anglia West because renewal work on track and signalling was more pressing at Cambridge, and was in hand in any event. Furthermore, the M11 motorway threatened BR's market and plans existed to transfer the 'Bed Pan' electrification team to Cambridge and the Hitchin–Peterborough section of the GN main line. By dealing with the short Cambridge–Royston section first it was proposed to divert main services to King's Cross to enable work to proceed on the Bishop's Stortford–Cambridge section. But the return on Anglia East was more attractive than the Royston–Cambridge section, leading the Department of Transport to give priority to the Norwich/Harwich routes and to reject Royston completely, although the Bishop's Stortford route gained belated approval in January 1984 after the deletion of electric multiple-unit depot facilities proposed at Cambridge. The Department gave qualified approval for Anglia East in December 1981, subject to continued viability of the proposals in the light of the reversed order of work. This was subsequently confirmed and final approval by the BRB for work to proceed was given in September 1982.

Anglia East was justified and approved principally on the basis of forecast increases in passenger

The Anglia projects owe their existence to the Advanced Passenger Train, for it was on the assumption that they would be in full service on the LMR, releasing electric locomotives, that the schemes were based. The ultimate withdrawal for scrap of some of the APT sets led one railway magazine editorial to suggest that shorn of some of their more troublesome innovations they could have served usefully on the London to Norwich line.

Above right: *Before the Anglia schemes could be justified, resignalling and track rationalisation had to gain approval. Wrabness was one of nineteen manual signalboxes rendered redundant under the Anglia East resignalling programme. However, this one lives on, having been moved to the preserved Colne Valley Railway. Mistley box enjoys a similar reincarnation at the Stour Valley Railway. Class 40s on the Mossend–Parkeston, like No 40 052 here on 6 November 1981, are also only a memory at this location.*

Right: *Almost everything in this picture, taken on 16 February 1983, was destined to be a thing of the past within five years. The pulleys and rodding would disappear when power signalling was extended from Colchester, as would Ipswich Goods Junction signalbox. The Craven's dmu blue asbestos content would see it doomed by 1987 at the latest, and the 22-year reign of Class 47 locomotives such as No 47 579, on Norwich trains would end with the completion of Anglia East in May 1987.*

Above: *No 37 040 takes a Harwich–Peterborough train out of Ipswich on 22 August 1983. The old semaphores can be seen in the distance. Track arrangement is from right to left down and up main, down and up East Suffolk lines.*

Above left: *No 45 009 heads the Mossend–Parkestone past Ipswich, with the rather less attractive array of new signals, on 14 December 1985. Note extension to Platform 3, removal of Goods Junction signalbox, ladder crossover to Upper Yard and other track alterations.*

Left: *No 47 581 at Ipswich with an up Freightliner on 6 June 1982, against the old array of semaphore and colour-light signals.*

No 47 576 heads a Yarmouth train at the same location as 37 040 above, on 8 September 1984. The masts have begun to encroach on the scene, the intrusive colour-light gantry has replaced the semaphores. The track has been rationalised, the locomotive passing the newly installed crossover to the singled East Suffolk line, third from the left.

revenue on the Harwich and Norwich lines. Even if only 70 per cent of the forecast increase in revenue were to be realised, the scheme was still viable. What gave the planners cause for such optimism? An important factor was East Anglia's position ahead of all other UK regions in the population growth league. Much of this is due to migration into England's most sparsely populated region. While much of this immigration consists of people above retirement age, the area has the third highest proportion of households in which the breadwinner is in a professional occupation. Clearly, they do not all commute to London, but Liverpool Street's ideal situation with respect to one of the country's unsung growth industries, the financial services of the City of London, had helped ensure gratifying passenger growth from earlier GE electrification schemes and this 'sparks effect' could reasonably be expected from the Anglia East improvements.

Though the London–Norwich line is second only to the East Coast Main Line in terms of passenger profitability, average family spending on rail travel in East Anglia is the lowest in the country. This fact together with the region's above average proportion of retired people means that there is a good potential market for off-peak optional travel which an electric railway can provide at much lower operating cost than with diesel.

On the defensive side, East Anglia ranks as the third region in the country in terms of car ownership. Ongoing improvements to the area's road network inspired by the growth of container traffic through Felixstowe and leading to the by-passing of Colchester, Ipswich and later Chelmsford, threatened abstraction of traffic from a rail service which had seen little improvement in the previous 20 years.

After Anglia East

With approval for Anglia East secured the planners were then able to look for spin-offs. The traction maintenance depot at Stratford had provided maintenance and servicing facilities for diesel multiple-units used on three services, Camden Road–North Woolwich, Romford–Upminster, and Wickford–Southminster. The third rail electrification of the North Woolwich line in 1985 meant that Stratford's facilities were required for the provision of just one unit for each single line branch – clearly an uneconomic situation, as was the alternative of transferring servicing and maintenance to Cambridge or Norwich. Largely on the basis of the savings inherent in removing dmu servicing facilities from Stratford, electrification of the Southminster branch was approved in January 1984, to be followed in June with a nod in the direction of the Upminster line.

But more significant developments were in the offing. A large proportion of GE-bound freight is hauled electrically down the West Coast Main Line, only to change locomotives at Willesden for diesel haulage over the North London line, sometimes just for the ten miles to Stratford Freightliner terminal. As well as extending transit times, this mitigates against intensive use of the diesel locomotives and their crews. So came a revival of the 1964 scheme to provide ac electrification over the North London line to permit through electric working onto the GE, only this time the route was Camden Road to Stratford. Coupled with relative small (though in some cases expensive) amounts of work at King's Cross Freightliner Terminal, Ipswich Upper Yard, Parkeston Quay, Ripple Lane, Dagenham Dock, Tilbury, and the 1½-mile link from Canonbury Junction to the ECML, the scheme will release five Class 47 and nine Class 37 diesel-electric locomotives for work elsewhere, allowing 443,000 annual train miles to switch to electric haulage. Significantly, this is the only project touching the GE area for which new rolling stock has been required, in this case four of the new Class 87/2 electric locomotives.

Looking to the future, the Felixstowe branch sticks out as an obvious candidate for electrification. The bulk of Felixstowe's traffic is on deep sea routes and is likely to be little affected by construction of the Channel Tunnel. Indeed the Dock company is sufficiently sanguine about growth prospects as to authorise the construction of a 1½-mile spur from Trimley into the dock, in order to avoid the series of level crossings mainly on dock premises, encountered by the present line.

The route was surveyed for electrification in 1985. The nine low road overbridges encountered as the line loops around the north-east side of Ipswich would cost some £2 million out of an overall figure for electrification and resignalling of £6 million. For 15¾ route miles (all single but for the three miles from East Suffolk Junction to Westerfield) this is expensive when compared with the £3 million cost of the 16-mile single line Southminster branch, but the earning potential of the Suffolk branch is incomparably greater. The Felixstowe scheme is in the process of evaluation, and as it is sponsored by the Freight Sector no provision is made for electrifying to Felixstowe Town terminal station. But when one considers that Marks Tey–Sudbury is on the electrification evaluation list for the future it is hard to imagine that the ¼-mile from Beach

The arms have been removed from all the semaphores as No 47 085 heads for Felixstowe over the singled East Suffolk line, the crossover to which is awaiting connection behind the second Freightliner flat. The train will regain double track once East Suffolk Junction is passed. Photographed on 9 April 1984.

Track rationalisation – 1: *Perhaps the site of one of the most drastic transformations in Anglia East, the view from Bramford looking towards Sproughton signalbox and the network of sidings, the further set of which is full of wagons for the British Sugar Corporation plant. No 47 114 passes with a Norwich train on 2 July 1977.*

Junction to the Town station at Felixstowe will not get the nod at some future stage, always assuming that the main scheme is approved.

Although under evaluation by the LMR, two future schemes could have great signficance for the GE. The LMR has an isolated pocket of dmu operation in the form of the Gospel Oak to Barking service over the old Tottenham & Hampstead line, and it is the elimination of this which may provide the justification for electrification of this route, the Woodgrange Park–Barking section of which is already wired, albeit at 6.25kV ac. At the same time the Region is considering a much more ambitious proposal involving the construction of a new junction between the Midland route and the North London line at West Hampstead in order to give access from the WCML via Willesden Low Level to the Snow Hill link to the Southern Region. Should the two plans come to fruition this would leave just

two miles of the North London line between Gospel Oak and West Hampstead innocent of catenary, the provision of which would enable freight bound for Barking and the LTS section to avoid the flat crossing of the four track GE main line at Forest Gate Junction, necessitated by the present route via Stratford.

Over on the west side of the Region an exciting new project gained Government approval in June 1986. It involves the construction of a new branch with triangular connections to the Cambridge line to serve Stansted Airport. Some of the 1½-mile branch will be in tunnel, but this and the cost of new terminal facilities are not the only factors contributing towards the £40 million bill, since for the first time since the 1960s a GE electrification is to be blessed with new rolling stock this time in the shape of five Class 317 units in addition to five refurbished Class 310 units with additional luggage space. Due to come into service in 1991, its trains will also serve new terminal facilities at the London end, since Liverpool Street should by that time have undergone its £80 million reconstruction.

By that time the Royston–Shepreth Branch Junction section may well have proved a case of

third time lucky and have got approval to permit through electric working between Cambridge and King's Cross. The case for this route may be strengthened by the strain on the double track line capacity which will be imposed by Stanstead Airport services on the Liverpool Street route.

It seems likely that Cambridge's role as a locomotive changing point may be short-lived, as the case for extending the wires a further 41¼ miles to King's Lynn is considered. Significant sections of this route have been singled and estimated costs are only £6.3 million, an average of £153,000 per mile compared with the £381,000 per mile of the Felixstowe branch.

In reviewing this impressive catalogue of actual and potential improvements, it is fascinating to see the key role of the original Anglia East and Anglia West projects in justifying further schemes. Under the chairmanship of Sir Peter Parker, the tendency was to try for Government approval for electrification on a network basis. The step-by-step approach now adopted has led to a similar end result, but each component part has had to be justified in its own right.

Since the formation of BR thirteen different schemes have contributed to the electrification of 360 route miles in the GE area, with the strong possibility of a further 71 miles being added in the not too distant future. The 1980s schemes approved so far have been responsible for 127 of these miles and have extended a suburban network into a main line one.

Electrification in GE Area
(all are 25kV ac unless otherwise stated)

Service started		Route	Route Miles
Sept	1949	Liverpool Street–Shenfield (1,500V dc)	20
June	1956	Shenfield–Chelmsford (1,500V dc)	10
Dec	1956	Shenfield–Southend Victoria (1,500V dc)	21
Apr	1959	Colchester–Clacton/Walton	24
Nov	1960	Liverpool Street–Shenfield (conversion to ac)	(20)
Nov	1960	Liverpool Street–Enfield/Chingford//Hertford East/Bishop's Stortford	46
Mar	1961	Shenfield–Chelmsford (conversion to ac)	(10)
June	1962	Chelmsford–Colchester	23
June	1962	London–Tilbury/Shoeburyness	74
May	1969	Clapton–Cheshnut	9
Oct	1977	Braintree–Witham	6
May	1985	Colchester–Ipswich	17
May	1985	Dalston Junction–North Woolwich (750V dc)	8
May	1986	Manningtree–Harwich	11
May	1986	Wickford–Southminster	16
May	1986	Romford–Upminster	4
Jan	1987	Bishop's Stortford–Cambridge	25
May	1987	Ipswich–Norwich	46
May	1988	Camden Road–Stratford (ac)	7

2 · Engineering Aspects

Track rationalisation – 2: (inset) *Ironically, most of the changed features at this location are not attributable directly to electrification. The removal of the sidings and the construction of Ipswich Western by-pass, the overbridge of which is seen here partially finished on 8 June 1984, would have happened anyway.*

Track rationalisation – 3: *The lamp standard to the right of the picture is that nearest the camera in the 1977 view (see page 22). No 31 414 passes under the completed Ipswich Western by-pass bridge in a blizzard on 7 February 1986.*

Electrical Systems

Since 1947, the GE area has experienced electrification at 650V dc third rail (this under London Transport auspices on the ex GE Essex branches), 1,500V dc overhead, 6.25/25kV ac dual voltage and 25kV ac.

In 1985 third rail 750V dc electrification was extended into GE territory with the energising of the Dalston Junction–North Woolwich route. Further extension of this system over former GE lines is due to take place in July 1987 with the opening of the Docklands Light Railway, though this system will involve current collection from the underside instead of the top surface of the third rail.

In the period significant advances in electrical engineering have reduced the safe clearances required for 25kV ac to the extent that it has proved feasible to eliminate dual-voltage working from virtually the whole of the GE area, only the sections from Forest Gate Junction to Barking, Fenchurch Street to Barking, and Leigh-on-Sea to Shoe-buryness remaining at 6.25kV. Ironically, having all but rid itself of voltage changeover points, the diversion of the Cross Town North London line services from Broad Street to Liverpool Street via the newly constructed Graham Road Curve in June 1986 brought back the need for dual-voltage stock, this time with the capability to switch from 25kV ac to 750V dc.

Electrical and Civil Engineering on the Early Schemes

The work of electrifying a stretch of railway is seldom limited to simply stringing up catenary, but almost always goes hand-in-hand with modifications to track and re-signalling. Track alterations take place to cope more efficiently with the new service; re-signalling will be necessary for this purpose and perhaps to provide closer headways. In these days of track circuiting it will also be necessary to immunise the signalling system from the traction current passing to earth through the rails, an operation which alone can add significantly to the cost of the project. Today's track alterations are likely to be in the nature of rationalisation aimed at removing redundant track and minimising expensive point and crossing work. Clearly while they are under way such major works are very disruptive to the running of services, and for obvious operational reasons track modification, re-signalling and electrification are carried out together wherever possible.

The Shenfield electrification was accompanied by major track alterations and bridgework in the vicinity of Liverpool Street, the provision of a flyover at Ilford (the first on the GE) and a major rebuilding of Stratford station to accommodate the London

Transport extended Central Line services and provide cross-platform interchange. Re-signalling from Liverpool Street–Shenfield saw the first application of a signal panel (as opposed to a power frame) at a London terminus. The work at Stratford included the provision of bay platforms for an electric shuttle from Fenchurch Street, aimed at maintaining a link with LNER services which had run thence out to Ongar and to Ilford and back via the Fairlop loop. Though wiring was installed from platforms 3 and 4 at Fenchurch Street to Stratford, no regular electric passenger service was ever instituted as it was felt that it would unnecessarily duplicate the extended Central Line service. Apart from use as a diversionary route during the East Coast floods of 1953 and for tests on the effect on clearances of the uplift of the wire when a train passed, the wiring can hardly have begun to pay for itself, a situation unlikely to recur these days.

The extension of the Shenfield electrification out to Southend and Chelmsford was accompanied by the construction of a burrowing junction at Shenfield so that the Southend trains did not conflict with the main line service. Seven pre-stressed concrete masts were installed experimentally between Rochford and Prittlewell, and in the same section the proximity of Southend Airport necessitated much closer spacing of masts in order to keep the overhead as low as possible. To increase visibility for aircraft crews the masts are painted alternately red and yellow.

While the use of the Clacton branch for trials of the 25kV ac system entailed no major civil engineering work it was vital as a test-bed for electrical engineering developments associated with the adoption of high voltage alternating current. The Styal line in Cheshire had been electrified on this system in 1956 primarily for the purpose of providing crew training facilities in advance of the Crewe–Manchester/Liverpool electrification and it was not used for public service until after the Essex electrification. The Clacton scheme was accompanied by re-signalling, since an important aspect of the test work involved studying the effects of high traction voltage on signalling and telecommunications.

The advantages of 25kV ac have already been mentioned, its drawback is the greater clearances required by the higher voltage. Where these would be prohibitively expensive to achieve, the reduced voltage of 6.25kV was authorised, necessitating the provision of voltage changeover facilities. In the light of the problems these were to cause on subsequent

Track rationalisation – 4: *The somewhat temporary nature of the signalling arrangements are evident in this view of 37 200 in Sproughton loop on the 8 June 1984. Construction of the overhead at this point had to await the removal of the loop which was needed while work continued in Ipswich Upper Yard.*

27

schemes it is perhaps unfortunate that the Clacton testbed was not used to try out the changeover equipment – it is easy to be wise after the event.

Many tests were carried out using the higher voltage, but the most bizarre of these took place at St Botolph's and involved a J20 steam locomotive and a dummy man. Unfortunately, a steam locomotive fireman had been electrocuted while working under overhead catenary and it had been claimed that the current had arced across a gap of nine inches. The experiment at St Botolph's was to prove that this could not have happened, but it was to have much further-reaching implications. The dummy was covered in graphite to represent the conductivity of the human body and was placed astride the boiler of the J20, whose crew was given instructions to make plenty of smoke. The overhead was then lowered and it was not until the wire was within 1¾in of the dummy that a flashover occurred. While initially the experiment served to provide reassurance to steam crews called upon to work under overhead wires, it was subsequently used to support the case for the first of the reductions in required clearances which, helped by advances in insulating materials, have significantly reduced the costs of electrification.

That there was no fear of unemployment at this time for the Region's engineers is evidenced by the work in hand at the start of the 1960s – conversion of Liverpool Street to Shenfield and on to Southend Victoria to ac and the opening of the North East London scheme, all put into public service in November 1960. While work continued on the conversion of the Shenfield to Chelmsford section to ac and its extension to Colchester to link up with the Colchester–Clacton/Walton section, the 74 route miles of the LTS route to Southend Central were also stretching resources to the limit.

Once the ac system had been decided on for the North East London and LTS routes, it was clearly desirable to convert the existing electrified routes to Southend Victoria and Chelmsford if intolerable operating inflexibility was not to be incurred. The adoption of the 6.25kV voltage for the Liverpool Street–Southend route obviated the need to raise bridges as existing clearances were adequate. The work was carried out without interruption to the weekday services.

The Shenfield to Chemlsford section was converted to 25kV ac and it proved necessary to substitute diesel units for electric units for a period of some months. While it proved possible to retain the four-year-old switchgear installed at supply points under the dc electrification it was necessary to substitute ac equipment at substations and track sectioning cabins, which involved the provision of new buildings as the dc equipment was required for operation until the final changeover.

The Chelmsford conversion was completed in March 1961 by which time the North East London scheme had been energised for four months, making it the first British electric railway to operate on the dual voltage ac system. Despite the adoption of the lower voltage from Bethnal Green to the environs of Cheshunt 44 bridges had to be rebuilt. The other major civil engineering work was the provision of new stations at Harlow and Broxbourne and the extension of platforms at most other stations on the route to handle the nine-car trains. Extension of multiple-aspect signalling out to Bishop's Stortford was accompanied by re-cabling to immunise the system.

The closing of the gap in the catenary between Chelmsford and Colchester was achieved in June 1962, and was accompanied by a major reconstruction of Colchester station and the provision of a burrowing junction for the Clacton branch.

Civil engineering work on an even grander scale was called for with the next electrification project, that of the former LTSR line from Fenchurch Street–Southend Central. At Barking, where the LTS traffic joined that of London Transport's District line to Upminster and the flow of mainly freight traffic from the Tottenham & Hampstead line bound for Tilbury, two flyovers to the west of the station and a diveunder to the east had to be constructed.

The LTS electric service began operating in June 1962 and the GE was to enjoy a breathing space before the next electrification work, the Lea Valley scheme over the nine miles between Clapton and Cheshunt, was completed in May 1969. While no major civil engineering work was involved, this section saw the first application of Mk III overhead line equipment. Compared to the Mk I equipment employed on all the post-Shenfield GE schemes this saw a reduction in the use of copper materials allied with the adoption of a smaller distance between the catenary and the contact wire. Headspan structures replaced the portal type at multi-track locations except in the vicinity of very poor ground.

Further cost reducing developments in overhead line equipment were employed on the Witham–Braintree electrification opened in October 1977. This employed the Mk IIIA equipment which had first seen use on the Weaver Junction–Glasgow section of the WCML. The catenary is made of steel-reinforced aluminium, and the distance between the contact wire and the catenary is reduced further.

While the Cross Town Link extension from Dalston to North Woolwich simply involved the provision of third rail, new stations at Dalston Kingsland and Homerton were provided with Greater London Council support and funding. The diversion of North London services from Broad Street to Liverpool Street involved the construction of a new piece of railway, the ¼ mile long Graham Road curve electrified at 25kV ac. The Class 313 dual voltage units employed on the route switch to third rail 750V dc at the Dalston Kingsland stop. The curve came into operation on 30 June 1986.

Anglia East Engineering, Planning and Execution

Anglia East was to be no exception to the rule of combining track and signalling modifications with electrification. Operationally it was particularly vital that all the work should be carried out at one fell swoop, since unlike some of the earlier suburban works there were no practical diversionary routes to cope with freight traffic, even if the alternative of carrying passengers by bus were to be employed. As has been seen, while operational dictates called for all the work to take place together, financial constraints meant that BR had to wait until the track and signalling work could stand on its own feet commercially before the financial case for electrification could be made.

The sequence of steps involved in planning an electrification gives an insight into the development of the Anglia East scheme.

Initially, a review of current traffic levels and the potential boost to traffic resulting from the 'sparks effect' is made. This then forms the basis for the operating department to formulate notional timetables from which the requirement for rolling stock, trackwork and other facilities may be determined. An overall survey of the route is then made to highlight particular problems and identify opportunities for track rationalisation. It is then possible to determine the level of power supply required and to plan the re-organisation or renewal of signalling.

The detailed planning work common to any electrification scheme can next be considered together with the actual decisions taken in the Anglia East scheme.

Following the overall survey, detailed inspections are then made to determine:

1. *Track alterations required.* For Anglia East this involved major track rationalisation at Norwich Thorpe and at Ipswich. Twenty-six sites requiring realignment for higher line speed were identified, of which the largest was at Needham Market.

2. *Bridges or tunnels requiring modification or rebuilding.* Fifty-four bridges needed raising to provide sufficient clearance, and even where this was not necessary parapets had to be raised to protect pedestrians from the overhead wires (or

Track rationalisation – 5: *Nos 25265 and 25256 demonstrate the need to remodel East Suffolk Junction as they pull out of Ipswich Upper Yard with returning Barham–Mountsorrel stone empties on 20 July 1982. Not only were the numerous crossovers expensive to maintain, but the lay-out made it difficult to accommodate 25 set Freightliners in the Yard.*

perhaps more significantly to protect the latter from the attentions of small and not so small boys intent on electrocuting themselves!) The troublesome Ipswich tunnel posed special problems. The rebuilding of Trowse Swing Bridge, though not included in the original submissions, turned out to be another example of the synergy provided by the Anglia East scheme.

3. *The need for rebuilding or modifying station buildings and other lineside structures.* Anglia East called for extensive facelifts at Ipswich, Stowmarket and Norwich stations.

4. *Location of feeder stations, track sectioning cabins, switching facilities and neutral sections.* Three new feeder stations and six track sectioning cabins, necessary to allow smaller sections to be isolated in the event of problems, were included in the programme.

5. *Siting of overhead line support structures.* 4,350 masts, requiring 1,550 tonnes of steel and 4,400 cubic metres of concrete foundations, were needed to support the 186 miles of contact wire used over the 130 track miles involved in the scheme.

6. *Location of new signalboxes, relay rooms and signal posts.* The separate track and signalling schemes mentioned earlier had made provision for a new power box at Colchester to become responsible ultimately for the whole of the area included in Anglia East, with the exception of Mistley to Harwich Town which was to be under the control of a satellite box at Parkeston. Nineteen manually operated boxes were thus rendered redundant. One hundred and fifty main signals, 200 points machines and 500 track circuits were required.

7. *Location of depots for engineering work.* The old locomotive depot at Ipswich was selected as a base for work not only on Anglia East but later on the Anglia West project also.

8. *Location of maintenance depots.* Since no new rolling stock was envisaged initially, the existing depot at Ilford was deemed able to cope with the more intensive use of its stock involved in the first two stages of the scheme. It would also be responsible for the day-to-day maintenance of the LMR based electric locomotives. Completion of the scheme through to Norwich saw the city's Crown Point depot wired for providing maintenance facilities at the northern end of the route.

9. *Where special arrangements need to be made, such as at level crossings or where power lines cross the track.* On the newly electrified routes 15 level-crossings were converted to automatic half barriers or remotely-controlled barriers.

10. *What wayleaves and easements are necessary.* The need to widen the embankment at Needham Market to ease the curves involved the purchase of land; the construction of the new Trowse Swing Bridge involved an Act of Parliament.

No 47 156 sets out from Ipswich Upper Yard with container flats for Felixstowe, passing one of the newly installed colour-light signals which spelt the end for East Suffolk Junction signalbox, from the gutted interior of which this picture was taken on 12 June 1984.

Above left: **Track rationalisation – 6:** *47 008 heads ballast hoppers as the new junction is installed on 8 April 1984. The signalbox was by then out of commission.*

Left: **Track rationalisation – 7:** *No 47 130 gingerly heads the first locomotive hauled passenger train onto the newly installed single East Suffolk line. The old crossovers are to the left of the locomotive. The new simpler crossover arrangement can be seen behind the second coach, opposite which the old semaphore post stands armless. The date is 9 April 1984 and the train is the 07.19 Lowestoft–Liverpool Street. The reconstructed Hadleigh Road bridge is in the background.*

With these details determined, the route must then be divided into suitable sections to enable sequence priorities to be determined and work allocated. All this forms the bare bones which the planners must dress with their estimates of costs and revenues for the detailed submission document, which must also give estimated completion dates. These should be as soon as possible both from the viewpoint of minimising interference with service operation, and to enable expensive capital equipment (which incurs interest charges from the outset) to start earning its keep at the earliest opportunity. Anglia East envisaged completion to Ipswich by May 1985 (which was achieved), to Harwich by December 1985 (which was not, services commencing in May 1986) and through to Norwich in May 1987.

A consideration of some of the special engineering problems of the Anglia East scheme serves to increase one's appreciation of the relatively smooth transition from diesel to electric traction which was achieved.

At one stage after the initial approval had been given it was decided to pare costs by singling nine miles of track north of Diss. Since only one freight on three days of the week uses the line between Diss and Trowse Lower Junction, and as there was no

BR's most photographed dmu, the prototype Sprinter unit, pays a promotional visit to the East Suffolk line on 9 November 1985. It was just left the single line section. The signalbox has gone and a substation marks the new order on the main line. To date, the masts by the leading cab of the unit are the last on the East Suffolk line, but surely it cannot be too long before the overhead is extended down the line to Felixstowe.

Ipswich Tunnel – 1: *One of the biggest engineering challenges of Anglia East was making Ipswich Tunnel fit for electrification. This involved the laying of slab track and necessitated single line working. The very wet conditions of the tunnel are seen here as No 47 487 leaves with a Norwich–Liverpool Street train on 15 July 1984.*

immediate prospect of more than two passenger trains each way in any hour, it was felt that double track was not necessary. Together with the savings on trackwork and catenary, it was hoped to achieve significant economies by centrally positioning the remaining track in the road bed and thus avoid bridge reconstruction at ten locations. In the event, it transpired that only one bridge would be amenable to such treatment. Singling would also have called for bi-directional signalling, and while the S&T department claimed that this could be done at no extra cost, there were those who had their doubts. Perhaps most significantly, if the speed advantage of the new form of traction were not to

Ipswich Tunnel – 2: *The structure gauging train arrived in Ipswich on the evening of 15 November 1984 to test clearances in Ipswich Tunnel after the laying of slab track. The structure gauging vehicle is marshalled between two support coaches (Laboratory 17 and 18), the front ends of which give very passable imitations of SR emu stock, although both are conversions from Mk 1 locomotive hauled coaches. Note that the crossover visible in the previous picture has been repositioned and is out of frame to the left.*

be lost, highly sophisticated (and expensive) pointwork would be required at each end of the single line. Various options were considered, which all presented problems until a French design of swing nose crossing seemed the only answer. The sole example of this type installed in this country is at Hitchin. It fails on average once per month and requires constant surveillance throughout the winter.

When the cost of removing one track and shifting the other was added to the equation, it was decided that the game was not worth the candle and the singling proposal was quietly dropped. Singling would have intensified the 'ripple effect' of late running which is not unheard of at Norwich on a summer Saturday with its inter-regional and cross-country trains, so the operators must have heaved a sigh of relief.

Ipswich Tunnel presented one of the greatest engineering challenges in Anglia East. When constructed in 1846 the land above contained few buildings and a cutting no deeper than that at Brantham could have been used. Some say that

Ipswich Tunnel – 3: *With work on the tunnel transferred to the up track, London trains used Platform 3, taking advantage of the newly installed reversible signalling. No 47 438 waits to leave on 23 September 1984, while the closure of the up line provides the opportunity for some track relaying in the station area.*

*No 08 752 heads the wiring train near **Halifax Junction** as the final stretch of overhead between **Ipswich Tunnel** and Colchester is completed on 5 August **1984 – a day when** Ipswich Tunnel was closed, enabling **the engineers to** enjoy full possessions outside the tunnel, too.*

Bruff, the engineer, had never built a tunnel before and chose this location to get some practice. His successors have wished heartily that he had chosen another site since there the terrain is glacial with gravel pockets occurring upredictably in the clay. One such, located above Ipswich Tunnel, permits water to permeate in large quantities through to the bore. To complicate matters, the tunnel is built on a curve and the two bores starting from either end did not meet squarely in the middle. Indeed, had electrification been authorised in the 1960s, there would have been insufficient clearance to meet the clearance requirements of the time. The development of Ipswich had led to quite dense residential building over the tunnel (to the extent that some of the capped ventilation shafts are located beneath houses!). Opening-out the tunnel was therefore not a viable option.

By the 1980s, slab (or paved concrete) track had been developed successfully from initial trials at

Radcliffe-on-Trent in 1969. It was used in 1974 in the Eglington Street tunnels in Glasgow to improve the electrical clearances as part of the WCML electrification scheme. By eliminating sleepers and ballast, slab track allows the accurate alignment of rails and significantly reduces line possessions for maintenance. Its high initial cost limits its application to tunnels and viaducts, particularly where overhead wiring adds to the problems of maintenance.

It was decided to lay slab track in Ipswich tunnel and this major exercise was to take place with no more than tour 24-hour possessions. The achievement of such a significant improvement without major disruption to traffic provides an

interesting example of the staging of work on such projects. It had been determined in the planning stages that bi-directional signalling between Halifax Junction and Ipswich station would significantly increase the flexibility of the rationalised track layout in the Ipswich area, and the provision of the new signals would considerably ease the single line working through the tunnel which would be necessary throughout its reconstruction. It was therefore necessary for the Ipswich track rationalisation work to be completed so that the new signalling could be installed. Only then could work on the slab track commence, though April 1984 had seen preliminary work on replacing the drainage in the tunnel in order to improve working conditions.

A special paving machine built and delivered in 1970 by Robert McGregor & Sons to fit the BR loading gauge, was installed to lay the second of the two layers of concrete to the very fine tolerances required. Special care was needed to avoid a repeat of the Penmanshiel Tunnel collapse in which the footings had been undermined, and the opportunity was taken to install resilient bearings in order to dampen the vibration of which tunnel-top residents had complained. Improved clearances enabled shields to be installed to protect the overhead from the dripping water, which at least was now more easily drained away. Completion of the work saw the arrival of the Derby gauge testing train on 15 November 1984. Clearances were pronounced satisfactory.

In 1985 BR had decided to adopt a 'big bang' approach to the remodelling of the complex Crewe network by shutting the system completely for six weeks. With Sunday travel taking a more significant market share, this was judged preferable to the interminable weekend possessions which offered the only alternative. The same solution was applied on a smaller scale to the remodelling of Norwich Thorpe. BR publicity proclaimed rather un-attractively 'We're clearing our throat at Norwich' and went on to explain that over the Easter Weekend, 28–31 March 1986, Norwich Thorpe station would be closed completely. Trowse station was renovated and called back into use. Most longer distance services which would normally have terminated at Thorpe were extended through to Yarmouth via the reinstated Wensum Curve, in order to avoid problems with reversal. The three platform faces coped remarkably well with a full service. Large numbers of staff were on hand to assist any passengers bewildered by the arrangements. A shuttle service of buses was used to link Trowse and Thorpe stations. The exercise was repeated on 3 August 1986 to permit further work in the Thorpe area to continue unhindered.

Perhaps the engineering project which most

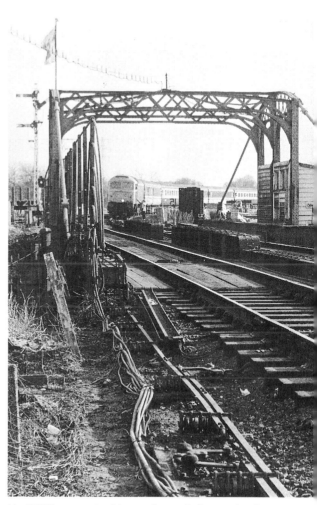

No 47 569 prepares to pick up a pilotman before crossing the Trowse Swing Bridge and taking the Wensum Curve with a Liverpool Street–Yarmouth train during the closure of Norwich Thorpe at Easter 1986. Note the semaphore arms for both directions on the same post.

Opposite: Norwich Throat – 1: No 47 579 leaves Norwich Thorpe with a train for Liverpool Street on 27 August 1983.

Norwich Throat 2: No 47 096 is at exactly the same spot, providing new ballast during the 'throat clearing' exercise, Easter 1986. The signalbox has disappeared and considerable track rationalisation has taken place.

captured the imagination was the replacement of the swing bridge over the River Wensum at Trowse. The first swing bridge dated back to 1846 and carried a single track. The bridge was doubled as part of a reconstruction in 1906 which utilised the foundations, bedplate, turning rollers and king pin of the original bridge. The present replacement was not involved in the original Anglia East submission, but the 1906 structure had been giving problems for many years and electrification posed a new challenge to the engineers, which could only be met satisfactorily by a new bridge.

There are few swing bridges on BR and Trowse was the first time that the problem of providing overhead electric power over such a structure had had to be faced. The engineers' initial reaction was to look to Holland, a country where electric railways and swing bridges are not uncommon. The Dutch solution was simple – don't worry about stringing wires across the bridge, simply let the trains coast over! Such an easy answer was out of the question at Trowse where up trains are starting from Thorpe station less than half a mile away, coming round a tight speed-restricted curve on a 1 in 344 uphill gradient. Banking of trains on this section would waste track capacity, while suspending the catenary independently of the bridge would have given insufficient clearance for shipping. A completely new approach to the problem had to be evolved. The old bridge was virtually life-expired and was slow in operation, as well as imposing a 15mph speed limit on trains crossing. It was therefore decided to build a completely new structure some yards upstream from the existing one. The current supply problem is overcome by the unique provision of a sort of overhead 'third rail'. From the landward sides of the bridge the ordinary catenary feeds into a fixed rigid rail on the non-moving sections of the bridge. These rails are tapered at their inner ends in order to meet, without actually touching, a similar rail over the track on the swinging central section of the bridge. Power for this movable section is provided by 25kV cables laid in trenches under the river bed and fed up through the pivoting point which is on the south bank. Return current travels via the locomotive wheels to the running rails, then through a cable up to the overhead structure and down via the trench to regain the current return rail on dry land. The fine tolerances required at the points where the pivoting central overhead rail comes close to the fixed rails meant that it was only practical to provide one track on the new bridge. Bi-directional signalling, faster operation of the swing section and a 40mph as opposed to a 15mph speed restriction should contribute to more flexible operation at this problem location. The greater clearances under the new bridge mean that it will need to be swung open less often for river traffic, but when it is a switch will be opened to disconnect the 25kV electricity supply from the overhead rail on the swinging section, in order to provide a completely safe passage for boats.

Although not used on the principal Anglia East electrification work, mention should be made of an important new technique of overhead mast erection which was first employed on an experimental basis on the 'add-on' Wickford–Southminster and Romford–Upminster sections. The idea originated from the BR staff suggestions scheme, and may turn out to be the most significant idea ever to originate from this source. The traditional method of mast erection involves digging and concreting holes which must then be left to dry before another possession is required to erect the masts. The new technique involves the use of heavy-duty steel tubes which are pile-driven straight into the ground by a vibrating piling machine. Masts then can be bolted to the top of the tube and the work completed in just one possession. In a given period twice as many such foundations can be laid as with concrete ones, with the added bonus that the masts can be erected at the same time. On the Southminster branch, where much of the work took place in freezing conditions, the added advantages of this new method were highlighted – earth no longer has to be removed, and there is no risk of the holes filling with water or caving in. Tubes of varying length are used to cope with different geological conditions. The new technique has been extensively used on the ECML electrification work where the need to minimise possessions has been paramount.

Throughout the post-war years the engineers have transformed much of the GE infrastructure, and it must be gratifying to them to know that in Trowse Swing Bridge and the new pile-driving method of mast erection they have been responsible for innovating techniques capable of wider application.

3 · Main Line Services

Introduction

The basic pattern of today's GE main line services was set in 1951 when the GE was blessed with the first allocation of the new BR Standard steam locomotives in the form of the Britannia Pacifics. At a stroke, the line's motive power leapt from a maximum of power class 5 provided by B1 and B17 4-6-0s to power class 7, and on the back of this came not only accelerated services but, more significantly, services provided at regular intervals, a boon for which passengers on many other lines had to wait until the advent of the High-Speed Train 25 years later. Summer 1950 had seen the introduction of the Clacton Interval Service and its principles were carried over to the 1951 Norwich line timetables, the 30 minutes past the hour departures from Liverpool Street then introduced persisting through to the present day.

Dieselisation in 1959 provided some acceleration, as did track improvements, but the best time for the London to Norwich run of 115 miles had only been reduced from 130 minutes in 1951 to 112 minutes by 1983, the last timetable before Anglia East electrification work started.

However, this period saw drastic changes wrought on the provision of train services in Norfolk and Suffolk. By the 1980s the main line service was confined to the London–Norwich axis only. No more did through trains run to Cromer or to Lowestoft, which towns were reduced to branch line status with shuttle services to the main line. The imminence of radio signalling on the East Suffolk line was used as an excuse for the withdrawal of the last through Lowestoft working in May 1984 (though Radio Electronic Tokenless Block working was not to come into full operation until February 1986) and the removal of the Wensum Curve at Norwich prefaced the virtual eclipse of through Yarmouth services (which had been diverted away from the East Suffolk route in 1966). For a while Yarmouth trains called at Norwich Thorpe and reversed, but the opening of Crown Point depot obviated the need to rely on the basic open-air stock maintenance facilities at Yarmouth and saw the through Monday–Friday service reduced to two trains each way daily by 1984. Thus the London–Norwich line had become the spinal cord providing connecting services at Norwich for Yarmouth and Cromer, at Ipswich for Lowestoft, Felixstowe and the Bury-St-Edmunds–Cambridge/Ely line and at Manningtree for Harwich (though the latter also had

its own through services from London and from Ipswich and points north).

When it comes to punctuality, a late-running connecting service is likely to have more serious implications than a through service when feeding onto the main line. A late through train coming off a branch can probably be fed into a path on the main line without causing delay to other services (depending on its subsequent stopping pattern) but when feeding into a main line connection that train must be delayed if the advertised connection is to be maintained. The problems are compounded on the Norwich line by through services joining the main line at the more southerly junctions, so that the

Overleaf: The lower top speed of the Class 86/0 and Class 86/3 locomotives meant that the LMR was more willing to release them to the GE for driver training than the front line Class 86/1 and Class 86/2. No 86 030 is seen at Ilford with a Thornton Fields–Colchester working on 20 November 1984. Training runs commenced on 30 October 1984. An early problem was encountered when No 86 316 ventured to the bufferstops at Liverpool Street and had to be hauled back by a diesel locomotive, having become electrically isolated as a result of years of grime accumulating on the contact wire at this point never reached by the pantographs of emus.

With four Class 86 locomotives based on the GE for driver training purposes, the opportunity was taken to employ them in revenue-earning service on a railtour which covered much of the then electrified GE area. On 2 February 1985, No 86 007 heads the erstwhile Manchester Pullman stock south of Bishop's Stortford on the final leg of the tour, providing a foretaste of Class 86 haulage on the Anglia West line which commenced in May 1987

density of traffic nearer London means that a late running Inter-City train can easily lose its path.

A total of 15 main junctions in a distance of 115 miles between Liverpool Street and Norwich averages out at one every 7²/₃ miles, a situation not encountered on any of the other main routes to London north of the Thames. The mix of traffic, with inner suburban stopping trains, outer suburban semi-fasts and express services to north of Colchester, must also accommodate important freight flows, the timekeeping of which is nowadays just as important as for passenger services.

It is against this background that the work of the train planner must be considered. If his job is seen as trying to squeeze a quart into a pint pot it might be said that the Anglia East electrification has increased the capacity of that pot by half a pint — though it may generate customer demand for a 'three pint' service!

Planning

As seen in Chapter 2, the train planners are involved at an early stage in planning an electrification project. Electrification must be justified in commercial terms, so the current performance and future potential of the route must be specified by the commercial section. This provides the basis for a notional timetable aimed at exploiting the line's potential. In turn the notional timetable enables estimates to be made of locomotive and rolling stock requirements as well as of the track facilities which will be required to meet the new service provisions. Even when no infrastructure improvements are in hand, the production of an ordinary timetable involves a lead time of 16 months, so that the planners must begin work on the next schedules before the first have gone into operation. With electrification, the time lag between the first notional table and the final public service timetable is even longer, and it is necessary to make constant revisions to traffic patterns in the light of changing circumstances. Furthermore, it is necessary to accommodate the work of the civil and electrical engineers on top of ongoing maintenance requirements on the route.

Meetings are held in January to prepare the timetable for the May of the following year. At these meetings compromises are thrashed out between the conflicting requirements of the business sectors and the maintenance departments. These 'rules of the route' meetings are followed by meetings at which the various sectors' business specifications are laid down and an attempt is made to match the supply of resources in the form of track, locomotives and rolling stock with the demand.

The train planners can now produce draft timetables. The computer at Derby will provide timings based on the route's motive power, rolling

stock and speed restrictions. The planners may seek to add new paths to the basic drafts, always trying to minimise the disruption on established services. With a rolling programme of electrification such as Anglia East the final improvements between Ipswich and Norwich beginning in May 1987 should have as little effect as possible on the new Harwich services (May 1986) and the electrified Ipswich–Liverpool Street service (May 1985). That the 30 minutes past the hour Liverpool Street departure times for Norwich trains have remained sacrosanct since 1951 is a measure of their success. The other constraints which must be accommodated are the turnround capacity of terminals, requirements for stabling and refuelling, maintenance, crew and manning requirements. With these added complexities, the notional timetable may well depart from the original commercial specification and it will then be necessary for further re-drafting to take place.

Electric Services

Computers have eased the burden on the train planner, but nonetheless his job remains a complex one. The problems may perhaps be highlighted by considering the introduction of the electrified services to Ipswich in May 1985. The commercial objectives were threefold: first, to accelerate the Norwich trains south of Ipswich; second, to satisfy the demand for an hourly fast service to Southend Victoria; and third, to provide fast trains at half-hourly frequency to Chelmsford and Witham, connecting with the Norwich services at Colchester. At this time line speeds were 50mph out of Stratford, 70mph to Ilford and then 80mph to Shenfield (60mph at Gidea Park in the up direction). After Shenfield the up road is limited to 70mph, while the down road has an 80mph limit until Chelmsford, where the curve through the station brings speed down to 60mph. Thereafter 100mph running is allowed until two miles south of Ipswich, apart from ¾-mile at 70mph through

First runs – 1: Class 305 units Nos 510 and 505 formed the first electric train to enter Suffolk under its own power when they were used for overhead line equipment tests between Manningtree and Ipswich on 9 April 1985. The train is seen at the county boundary formed by the River Stour at Manningtree.

Inset left: *Service reductions in 1983 saw BR take the opportunity to withdraw some emus with blue asbestos insulation. No 305435 was among a batch retired at this time. It was renumbered 305935 in departmental stock to serve as an instruction unit ahead of electrification and is seen in this role in Ipswich Upper Yard on 21 October 1984. The unit subsequently visited Harwich and Cambridge.*

Inset right: **First runs – 2:** *Heads peer out of the rear windows of No 86 259 as it gingerly negotiates the wiring in Ipswich Station yard for the first time. This was the first electric locomotive to reach Ipswich unassisted which accounts for the audience on 11 April 1985.*

First runs – 3: *With orange-jacketed BR officials very much to the fore, No 86 214 arrives at Ipswich on 29 April 1985 with a test train. The audience had gathered to witness the locomotive changing trials. Perhaps as a result of stage fright this took 17 minutes as opposed to the scheduled eight.*

First runs – 4: *No 86 324 arrives at Ipswich on a driver training trip on 23 April 1985, extended at short notice from Colchester. To date this the only Class 86/3 to reach Ipswich unassisted, although No 86 311 was hauled through en route to Crown Point Open Day in September 1983.*

First runs – 5: *The first passenger-carrying electric service to reach Ipswich was a press run to demonstrate the newly refurbished Class 309 unit No 605, here at the rear of a formation consisting of Nos 621 and 624 on 17 April 1985. The train is about to enter Ipswich Tunnel and is running alongside the new retaining walls built to prevent embankment slippage. In the middle distance can be seen the old Ipswich MPD, now serving as a base for electrification work. The Orwell Bridge in the background adds to the transformation of the Ipswich transport scene.*

First runs – 6: *The first diesel to electric changeover on a public service train takes place at Ipswich on 1 May 1985 as No 47 582 runs back from Halifax Junction having brought in the 10.17 from Norwich. No 86 259 backs on for the run to Liverpool Street. Such locomotive changes were soon being accomplished very smoothly; indeed on one occasion enthusiastic staff had jumped down and uncoupled a Class 31 locomotive from a Harwich train before realising that it was booked to work throughout!*

Manningtree. By May 1985 engineering work on the section between Norwich and Ipswich was in full swing and midday single-line working added 15 minutes to the overall timings. Other speed orders for permanent way slacks on the route made it necessary to add a further nine minutes to the schedules of all trains. Locomotive changing at Ipswich added eight minutes in the down direction and 12 minutes going up since, in the case of London-bound trains, the diesel locomotive coming off could only get out of the path of the train by proceeding through Ipswich Tunnel and awaiting a path to cross onto the down line at Halifax Junction.

In the evening peak between 17.00hrs and 18.00hrs, 60 trains had to be found paths over the six tracks out of Liverpool Street. Twenty-four of these departures took the Cambridge line at Bethnal Green, leaving 36 for the four tracks through Stratford to Shenfield. The slow lines accommodate a service consisting basically of all stations to Gidea Park and all stations to Shenfield. The fast tracks carry a Southend service with a first stop off the main line at Billericay; it then proceeds all stations to Southend Victoria, with express services for destinations beyond Shenfield on the main line running non-stop at least as far as Shenfield. A second Southend service illustrates well the constraints facing the train planner. Commercial requirements call for a 20-minute service stopping at Stratford, to provide cross-platform interchange for Central Line commuters, and at Harold Wood, then all stations to Southend. This requires running slow line to Stratford then fast line to Gidea Park Junction before switching back to the slow line for the Harold Wood stop. 25mph restrictions on the crossovers eat further into valuable fast line paths into which 21 peak hour services must be squeezed. The problem is compounded by rolling stock limitations. The Class 307s on the Southend service have a 75mph maximum speed, so their slower acceleration from the crossover slacks and inability to make full use of the 80mph fast line speed inhibit the full exploitation of the higher speed capabilities of the Class 309s, Class 312s and Class 86s providing fast line services to Chelmsford and beyond.

The need to allow for engineering works on the line north of Ipswich destroyed the integrity of the even interval departure pattern from Norwich, the 17 departures for London leaving at nine different minutes past the hour. While departures south from Ipswich were more standardised, there were 15 different time allowances for the 25 services, which were only partly accounted for by the eight different stopping patterns.

The 1986 Summer Timetable showed even more variation in Norwich departure times with 11 different minutes past the hour for the 17 services. This was partly due to an acceleration of services

as the remaining engineering work became concentrated on fewer sites, allowing most schedules to be speeded up. Between the peaks trains were 17 minutes faster to Ipswich. Departures south from Ipswich were subject to only slight alterations in a few cases, the main change being that the two-hourly emu stopping service now left at the odd rather than the even hours. The variability of departure times and time allowances persisted.

Harwich was the main beneficiary of the 1986 timetable, which saw the first electric services reaching the Harwich port. Advertised daily through services to Parkeston Quay were quadrupled from two to eight, with seven in the up direction, while the speed of the fastest service rose from 46.4mph to 53.3mph.

The restoration of through locomotive working between London and Norwich consequent upon the completion of the Anglia East programme saw the opportunity taken to restore the even interval service pattern. Now the concept has been taken to its logical conclusion, since not only do trains leave terminals at a standard number of minutes past the hour but they follow a standard stopping pattern, so that all the main intermediate stations benefit.

The 'Parkway' concept had been extended to Manningtree in 1985 when new and much enlarged car parking facilities were provided. The 1987 electric service to Norwich was designed to exploit further the high level of car ownership in East Anglia for the benefit of the railway by seeking to develop the potential of Stowmarket and Diss to serve as railheads for a wide area. The hourly Norwich trains now follow a standardised stopping pattern (Colchester, Manningtree, Ipswich, Stowmarket, Diss) so the service can be promoted as a two-hour transit from Norwich, with Stowmarket and Diss benefitting not only from a 25-minute faster service but one which runs every hour instead of the previous somewhat random pattern which the casual traveller perceived. Such a regular service pattern has the added advantage of economising on one set of stock.

The line's 'flagship', the East Anglian, is the only service to buck this trend, stopping only at Ipswich to achieve a London arrival in 100 minutes. All the Norwich trains will be in the hands of Class 86 electric locomotives with the exception of the last service south, which sees a welcome improvement on the 20.00 departure time in the previous timetable to a much more reasonable 22.55. This is worked by a Class 309 unit.

The Service in Practice

It has to be admitted that electric services to Ipswich were not without their problems in the first two years. Initially this could be put down to unfamiliarity

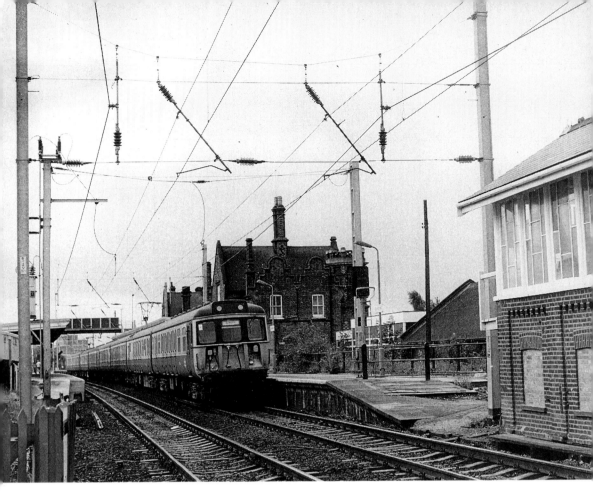

with the new equipment, some drivers being wary at first of the rheostatic braking on the Class 86 locomotives. With Willesden depot retaining custody of the locomotives and carrying out Class E examinations there was a suspicion that the GE might not always have received locomotives in peak condition. Certainly there were failures and days when diesels had to be called in as replacements, since there were simply insufficient serviceable electrics on the GE. (Despite strong lobbying, the GE was unable to obtain its own allocation of electric locomotives. Perhaps in part this was because the ability of Willesden more easily to maintain locomotives used on the GE was one of the arguments used to justify the North London electrification!).

However by 1986 one would have hoped that such problems might have been resolved. Instead, dissatisfaction from various travellers' representative bodies reached a peak, intensified no doubt by disappointment that the new service did not seem to be 'delivering the goods'. Studies by BR could unearth no statistically significant persistent cause or causes – indeed, many of the problems arose from factors outside BR's control, lineside fires and power failures being responsible for major disruptions on several occasions.

The nature of the route with its frequent junctions has been mentioned already. An illustration of the operating difficulties these can cause was highlighted by a local travellers' organisation's claim that the 06.38 Norwich–Liverpool Street had amassed a total of 53 hours lateness between May and December 1985, an average of nearly 19 minutes every day. From Manningtree this train was booked to run behind the 07.40 Parkeston Quay–Liverpool Street, which often got off to a late start itself due to awaiting ferry connections. The Norwich train was retimed two minutes earlier away from Ipswich to gain a path ahead of the boat train.

Not all the problems can be so readily solved, and unfortunately it is the case that these days modernisation can only be justified in terms of economy in men and capital. Rationalisation of track, rolling stock and motive and man power exact a price nonetheless by making the railway less able to cope with out-of-course emergencies arising from such mundane causes as staff illness or equipment failure. At least the authorisation for the building of new electric locomotives for the East and West Coast Main Lines should go some way to easing the chronic locomotive shortages, which have done nothing to enhance the Anglia East performance.

It seems unlikely that BR will ever get the chance to build a completely new railway from scratch, a luxury enjoyed by several foreign railway administrations. Consequently, in this country, new

First runs – 8: *Class 308 units were used for the overhead line equipment tests on the Harwich branch and units Nos 141 and 151 are seen near Bradfield on one such run on 14 April 1986.*

Above left: **First runs – 7:** *Class 312 units Nos 798 and 786 were used to inaugurate the electric passenger service from Stowmarket to Liverpool Street and are seen in the refurbished station waiting to form the 07.13 to Liverpool Street on 5 August 1985.*

305450 and 308991 on overhead line equipment trials over the Upminster branch on 13 April 1986. As the branch is worked under one train operation rules, the yellow light on the end of the platform at Romford marked the division between station limits and the single line proper since two electric units were on the branch at the same time.

Locomotive change at Ipswich. No 47 582 arrives with the 10.17 from Norwich to Liverpool Street and will be detached while electric locomotive No 86 259 waits alongside ready to take over on 1 May 1985.

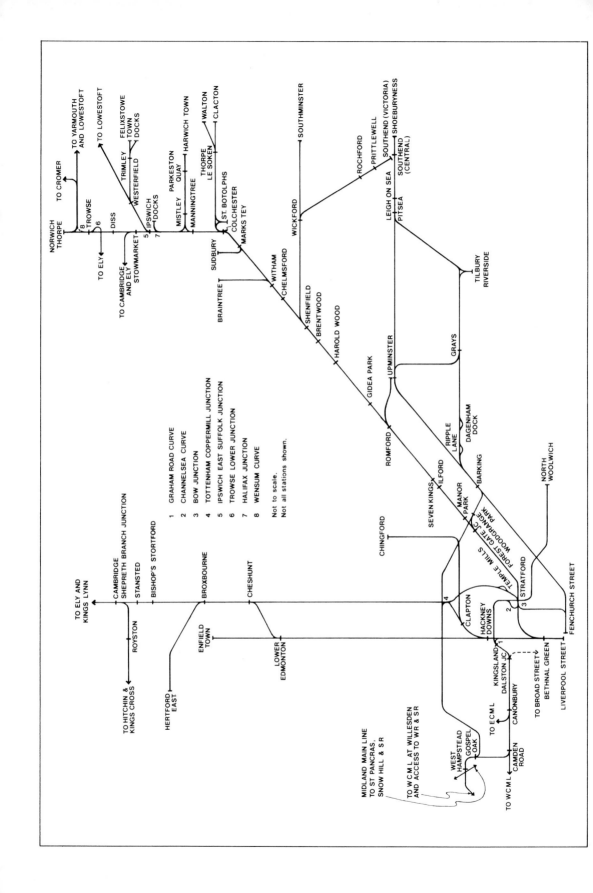

Map of Anglia East and associated lines

First runs – 9: *Emus Nos 305510 and 307104 work on an overhead line equipment test train down the Southminster branch, and have just left the remote Fambridge station on 23 March 1986. The Class 305 unit may have been providing insurance against the dewirements to which the Class 307 was prone. The latter type, however, seems to have settled down on the branch.*

First runs – 10: *No 86 255 was the first electric locomotive to work on the Harwich branch on 15 April 1986 when it was used for testing all crossovers and sidings, being more flexible for this purpose than emus. It is seen here at Mistley.*

and improved equipment has to function with an ageing infrastructure often intensifying the pressure on the superannuated plant, the signalling between Stratford and Gidea Park being a case in point. The cabling is more than 40 years old and the cross-currents set up when water penetrates worn gutta percha covering has contributed to the signal engineers' ulcers. It has also probably contributed to more than one fire which has immobilised Liverpool Street during peak periods.

One can only hope that the significant progress made by BR in reducing the claim on government grants towards running costs (all the more impressive when it is remembered that all the current electrification schemes in England are funded from BR's own resources) will be rewarded by money being made available to cover depreciation, without which the potential of the new schemes cannot be fully realised.

The Southminster scheme has shown most dramatically how electrification can boost traffic. Peak hour through trains are often full before they come off the branch at Wickford, and consideration is being given to extending the platforms at the branch line stations (for the second time in three years) to accommodate 12-car trains.

Ironically, similar success from a completed Anglia East could prove an embarrassment since line capacity is almost fully utilised between Colchester and Shenfield in the peaks. Of the six intermediate stations only one (Witham) has passing loops and, while the diversion of 75mph emus away from this section will increase line capacity it will be to a somewhat marginal extent. The ingenuity of the train planners will be put fully to the test in devising a service pattern which meets the needs of the intermediate stations without unduly inhibiting the express services. For the next three years these problems will be exacerbated by the reconstruction work at Liverpool Street which will also mitigate against the use of longer train formations to increase capacity. One day passing loops might be constructed at some of the intermediate stations between Colchester and Shenfield or, more dramatically, bi-directional signalling permitting 'one-way traffic' over both tracks during peak periods. One thing is certain; the completion of Anglia East will not see the end of the railway's response to new challenges in this part of the country.

Indeed as this book was in preparation it was announced that full resignalling between Bethnal Green and Colchester was due to start at the end of 1989 with the likelihood that the Shenfield to Colchester bottleneck would indeed enjoy bi-directional signalling.

4 · Locomotives and Rolling Stock

While to the casual observer electric locomotives first appeared on the GE scene in 1985, the area's association with electric locomotives is in fact much longer-lived. 1949 saw the first electric locomotive to work on GE metals, the only such machine to this day to be permanently allocated to a GE depot, Ilford. Perhaps foreseeing future development, Ilford was loth to let the locomotive out of its sight and No 26510's work as depot shunter saw it confined to the shed's precincts for the latter part of its life on the GE. No 26510 started life in 1914 when it had been built as North Eastern Railway No 11, to haul coal trains on the Newport–Shildon line. The Depression of the 1930s saw this traffic so badly hit that the line was one of the earliest (and certainly the largest) examples of de-electrification, foreshadowing the closure of the Woodhead route by 46 years when the overhead wires were switched off in 1935. Parallels with the Woodhead line did not end there. LNER No 6498, as No 11 had become, spent a long period in store together with its nine sisters. Consideration was given to using them as bankers on the Woodhead route before No 6498 was refurbished prior to despatch to Ilford for working in the new car sheds in August 1949, when it was renumbered 26510.

While perhaps not quite in the class of the 'Railway Race to the North' No 26510 participated in stimulating if somewhat unofficial trials during its early days on the GE. When brash new Class EM1 locomotives Nos 26001–3 were sent to Ilford for commissioning and driver training purposes, Ilford depot staff could not resist the temptation to see how the veteran NER machine would stand up against the newcomers. With line occupation less intense in those days, there was more than one occasion when No 26510 on the down electric line would be lined up against an EM1 on the down main at Seven Kings and battle would commence up Brentwood bank to Shenfield, with the 36-year-old locomotive giving a very good account of itself!

All too soon, such invigorating outings came to an end and 26510 retired to Ilford depot, its most notable experience thereafter being its renumbering into departmental stock as No 100 in January 1959. It was then stored at Goodmayes from June 1961 to February 1964, and finally moved to Doncaster for scrapping in mid-1964.

The GE's other associations with electric locomotives have been of a much more transitory nature. One actually pre-dates the arrival of No 26510, occurring in September 1947 when Woodhead Class EM1 prototype No 6000 (originally LNER No 6701 and later BR No 26000) blazed a trail which was later to be followed by its EM2 cousins when it travelled via Harwich to join the Zeebrugge train ferry for Holland in order to gain working experience denied it in this country by the lack of a suitably electrified line. It returned by the same route in March 1952 and was named *Tommy* at Liverpool Street station in June before going to Gorton for overhaul prior to making its much delayed debut on the route for which it had been designed originally. As has been mentioned, *Tommy*'s production batch derivatives also visited the GE. With the Shenfield electrification in operation, it was no longer necessary to seek overseas co-operation in testing the new locomotives and Nos 26001–3 were sent to Ilford. There they ran trials to Shenfield and back in November 1950 testing current collection, regeneration and air brakes, both light engine and with nine passenger carriages as well as double-headed on a train of 44 loaded locomotive coal wagons, which involved restarting on Brentwood bank. Possibly the successful outcome of this latter exercise convinced the authorities that the banking assistance of the antique EB1s would be superfluous (*ante*). Nos 26001–3 were joined by Nos 26004–10 and were used for driver training purposes until being despatched north when the first section of their intended route, from Wath to Dunford Bridge, opened in early 1952.

No 27002 of the express passenger Co-Co EM2 version of the EM1 class, pioneered the way south, later to be followed by the rest of its class. In March 1956 it appeared at Southend Central in an exhibition to celebrate the centenary of the completion of the LTSR. Thirteen years later, in September 1969, all seven EM2s, rendered

Overleaf: *With the usurpers lined up for the takeover on the following Monday, Class 47 No 47 582 leaves Ipswich on the last Saturday of regular diesel operation to Liverpool Street, 11 May 1985.*

Inset: *Two former Woodhead dc electric locomotives visited the GE when they returned from Holland for preservation on 15 July 1986. They are seen in Harwich Town yard awaiting tripping to Parkeston by Railfreight liveried No 31 252.*

redundant by the diversion of passenger services between Manchester and Sheffield off the Woodhead route, travelled to Harwich en route to Holland where all but one (which was cannibalised for spares) enjoyed a life span almost equal to, and in some cases greater than, that they had had on BR. Final withdrawal of the class came in 1986. Two were saved for preservation and again trod GE metals when NS No 1502 (ex No 27000) and No. 1505 (ex No 27001) returned via Harwich en route for Butterley and Bury (Lancashire) respectively.

Other visits to the GE by dc locomotives have also been associated with the end of their lives on BR. Southern Region Class 71 Nos 71 004/9/10/11/13/14 spent about a month in mid 1979 stored in Temple Mills yard before despatch to Doncaster for breaking-up. One other of the type was also scrapped at Doncaster and may have travelled via the GE, which prototype No 71001 certainly did en route to the ex GN works for restoration prior to preservation at the National Railway Museum.

The Southern's electro-diesels have occasionally penetrated GE territory. Records include No 73 106 at Lea Bridge as long ago as 1974. In November 1985, No 73 140 joined No 33 211 in hauling five withdrawn Hastings demu cars to Temple Mills for onward despatch to Mayer Newman's scrapyard at Snailwell. In both cases the locomotives concerned were of necessity on diesel power, but in February 1985 a Class 73/1 locomotive was able to take advantage of the third rail in GE territory when it worked a train of two 4TC units to North Woolwich in electrification proving trials.

London Transport's ex Metropolitan Bo-Bo electric No 12 attended the open day at Stratford in 1983 and, as far as is known, this completes the catalogue of dc electrics to visit GE metals.

The history of ac types on GE Lines is inevitably shorter. A quite frequent visitor has been ADB968021 (ex No 84009), the mobile load bank which first appeared in the area in Autumn 1980 in association with newly converted 25kV overhead between Liverpool Street and Gidea Park, which was the last part of the Liverpool Street to Southend route to be energised at the higher voltage. The commissioning of this section also led to the first ac locomotives to work on their own power on the GE when Nos 86 001 and 86 008 visited the Southend line in January 1979. No 86 244 went to Clacton to participate in the inauguration of the new electric

Although electric services were extended to Stowmarket within three months of reaching Ipswich in 1985, the latter point was the natural place for locomotive changing and Norwich trains continued under the wires, but with diesel traction for the following two years. No 47 580 is seen passing Claydon on 4 January 1986. The photograph is taken from the up platform of the closed station. Moves to restore the station here and at Finningham seem doomed to failure, with Diss and Stowmarket selected as railheads.

depot in July 1981 and No 86222 was at the same venue to help celebrate the centenary of railways at Clacton in 1983. No 87004 was at Stratford's first open day in 1979, while No 86224 attended the same function in July 1983 and No 86311 became the first workable ac electric locomotive to penetrate Suffolk and Norfolk when it was hauled to Crown Point's open day in 1983. Thus nine different electric locomotive types visited the Great Eastern before inauguration of the first stage of Anglia East in 1985 saw the regular employment of Class 86 locomotives on passenger services in the area.

Visiting emus

In Chapter 2 the various electrical systems used in the GE area were discussed. One such system was not mentioned since it was never employed in public service, but its use for test purposes in March 1956 allowed the Fenchurch Street–Bow Junction section to do a little more to justify its existence and provided the GE with its first visiting emu.

In the early 1950s, French success with ac traction had prompted BR to re-equip the Lancaster–Morecambe and Heysham line as a testbed for ac at 6,600 volts and 50 cycles/second. Originally electrified by the Midland Railway in 1908 (the first ac electric service in the country) the system had initially operated at the same voltage but at 25 cycles and had been de-electrified when it became life-expired in 1951. To operate the new service, which began trial running in November 1952 and was opened to regular passenger service in August 1953, three 3-car sets which had started life as fourth-rail dc units on the Willesden to Earl's Court service in 1914 and had been stored since the withdrawal of that service in 1940, were made available and were later joined by a fourth set. Various rectifiers were tested on the stock in its new ac guise, but the most significant of these was the germanium rectifier developed by British-Thomson-Houston. This was tested in the motor coach of one set on the Lancaster–Morecambe line before the trials were transferred to the Fenchurch Street–Bow Junction section where the overhead was fed at 6,600V ac for the period of tests which were concerned to establish safe clearances.

The London Midland Region was also to provide the next emus to visit the GE, when in 1962 eight Class 304 units were sent to the rescue of a GE in the throes of transition to dual voltage ac power. They were mainly employed on the Liverpool Street–Southend and Chelmsford services. April 1979 brought a visitor from another region, this time the Southern, when 4EPB unit No 5358 fitted experimentally with B4 bogies on its trailer cars was paired with a native Class 302 set which had received Class 312 bogies for test purposes, the whole unlikely ensemble being hauled over LTS lines by a Class 47 diesel-electric locomotive.

A surprising visitor in April 1982 was Watford dc line Class 501 unit No 154 which was hauled into Liverpool Street for clearance tests before retiring for maintenance at Ilford, suggesting that consideration may have been given to bringing the third rail into Liverpool Street when the diversion of services from Broad Street was originally envisaged.

The extension of the dc conductor rail to North Woolwich in 1985 saw dc units as a regular feature on GE metals. Early tests in February 1985 brought a Southern Region Class 73 and a 4VEP unit to the line, and it was reported that the 4VEP unit also ran alone. The commencement of electrified passenger services saw rather more basic 2EPB units provided, their spartan interiors not enhanced by the bars across the door droplights, made necessary by the tight clearances in Hampstead Tunnel.

The GE's skill in the paintshop is not confined to Stratford DRS and July 1986 saw GN Class 317/2 No 317368 at Ilford for painting in the new Network South East livery, giving the GE a foretaste of a type destined to enter service on the Cambridge line on the completion of the Stansted Airport branch.

With the visit of preserved SR 4COR unit No 3142, travelling via the GE from its original retirement home on the Nene Valley Railway to Brighton on 2 September 1986 and the Docklands Light Railway units entering service in July 1987, a total of nine visiting emu types can be added to the area's indigenous fleet in the period since 1949, and this is not to mention the London Underground stock running over former GE lines in Essex. Various withdrawn units including LT District Line CO/CP stock, Merseyrail Class 502 units, Glasgow 'Blue Train' Class 303s and SR 2HAP units have all visited March or Snailwell on their last journeys.

GE Motive Power Policy

When the Anglia electrification schemes were under consideration it was fondly believed that the LMR would be playing host to a fine new fleet of Advanced Passenger Trains by the time East Anglia required electric locomotives. This would have released more than sufficient locomotives for the Anglian schemes, continuing the policy of cascading stock eastwards which has operated since the GE received its last brand-new locomotive in the form of No D6729 in 1961. Gone were the days when the GE section had been selected as the first recipient of

Class 309 electric units reached Parkeston sooner than envisaged, when due to rolling stock shortages they were used to form extra boat trains during the summer of 1985. They were hauled between Parkeston and Colchester by Class 37 diesels. No 37 097 is seen at Parkeston with Class 309 emus Nos 614/6/7 on 10 August 1985.

Few stretches of line can have undergone so many changes of status as the Wensum Curve. Re-instated in 1986 to ease the problems of Thorpe Station closure, it was also used by certain Summer Saturday trains before being once again closed, only to re-open to provide turning facilities for dmus. The radio fitted East Suffolk unit seen at the rear of this train is on a 'throat clearing' diversion from Trowse–Lowestoft on 29 March 1986.

Above: *Boat trains, such as this DFDS charter seen behind No 47 518 at Bradfield on 28 March 1986, are something of a mixed blessing. The irregular nature of the sailings require separate pathing operations each time, and late docking of the ships can have serious repercussions on the rest of the system.*

Left: *No 47 570 passes Crown Point depot as it takes the re-instated Wensum Curve with a diverted Liverpool Street–Yarmouth train at Easter 1986. No 47 096 waits with ballast for the relaying operations at Thorpe on 29 March 1986.*

BR's new standard steam locomotives, the Britannia Pacifics. If the Railway Executive had been seeking to improve the prospects of acceptance of the new standard types by sceptical locomen by ensuring that they transformed services on their first allocation, they could not have chosen better than the GE lines whose passenger trains up to that time were innocent of motive power beyond power class 5. By the end of the 1950s the GE was also in the vanguard of dieselisation, receiving the first batches of what were to become Classes 31, 40 and 37. The fact that by then a considerable portion of the London end of the GE lines was under catenary may have contributed to the decision to favour the area with further new investment. By then, advances in the design and manufacture of overhead equipment had extended the life span of copper contact wire to 100 years, yet in some locations smoke and steam contamination was causing the need for renewal every three years as well as calling circuit breakers into operation with greater frequency. Furthermore, the fireman's job was made particularly hazardous by the presence of overhead wires. Many of the area's workings were

self-contained and these factors, coupled with the dynamism of Line Traffic Manager, W. G. Thorpe, saw East Anglia become the first part of the country to be completely dieselised.

Since then new rolling stock has been increasingly hard to come by as the accelerating motorway building programme in other parts of the country diverted BR's increasingly scarce investment resources to defensive responses on the lines threatened by the new roads. Since the mid-1960s, the GE's only new rolling stock has been 19 Class 312 and 61 Class 315 electric units.

The Anglian electrification submissions avoided the significant cost of new motive power by relying on more intensive use of existing electric units and providing for the cascade of surplus WCML locomotives. Initially, it was envisaged that the LMR Class 81s would be transferred to the GE en bloc, but the poor performance of this first of four prototype ac classes saw the decision switched in favour of Class 86. The Class 81 locomotives would have been 25 years old by the time they were needed for GE service, and although the Class 86 machines were only five years younger the BR broadsheet issued to keep travellers abreast of Anglia developments showed the fine art of PR in making a virtue of necessity when it headlined one article 'GE to get proven locomotives'! The original announcements had spoken of refurbished Class 86/4 locomotives being used on the Great Eastern, but in the event since part of their refurbishment involved the provision of fittings for multiple working, the LMR decided that they were too valuable to lose and offered Class 86/2 instead.

Norwich Trowse station was called back into use whilst Thorpe was closed during the 'throat clearing' operations at Easter 1986. Most main line trains were extended to Yarmouth to avoid problems with running round at Norwich. Class 47 No 47 497 is seen arriving at Trowse with the 09.44 Yarmouth–Liverpool Street on 29 March 1986.

The first day of full electric services on the Harwich branch, 12 May 1986, finds No 86 249 on the down Day Continental at Bradfield. The eleven-mile branch must see more named trains than any other line on BR with the Day, Hook and Essex Continentals, the European and the North West Dane (Blackpool–Parkeston), perhaps reflecting an attempt by BR to convince the EEC that it was getting its moneys-worth from the Transport Commission's grant towards electrification, given for facilities which further transport links with Europe! From the May 1987 timetable, the Day and Hook Continentals are renamed the Benjamin Britten and the Admiral de Ruyter.

No 86 246 heads the 09.40 Norwich–Liverpool Street over the River Stour at Manningtree on 27 July 1985.

Above: *Whilst it proved possible to get one complete rake of coaches into the new livery in time for use on the first electrically-hauled East Anglian, trains of mixed liveried stock persisted for some time on other services as can be seen in this picture of No 86 222 on the 16.30 Liverpool Street–Norwich at Brantham on 3 July 1985.*

A two-car Metro Cammell unit crosses the new Trowse Swing Bridge on its first full day of operation, 16 February 1987. The overhead power supply rail has yet to be installed. The bridge pivots from the south (far) bank.

Class 86

The 100 Class 86s were the second generation of ac electric locomotives developed from the experience gained from the initial 100 locomotives of Classes 81-85. Introduced in mid 1965, at least four years' experience had been gained of the preceding classes. Many of the changes introduced on Class 86 were beneficial, such as the adoption of 45in as opposed to the 48in diameter wheels of the earlier types. This allowed greater headroom in the locomotive body and improved the working environment. The adoption of automatic rheostatic braking realised the potential savings which the manual control used on the earlier Class 85 had condemned to idleness. Under this system, the traction motors are set automatically for braking causing them to become generators. As the current through the motor field coils increases, the magnetism across the motor armatures rises causing them, and thus the locomotive wheels, to slow down. Unlike regenerative braking, the energy thus created is not fed back into the overhead but is dissipated as heat. Ordinary air braking is employed when speed drops below 20mph, but the system gives the advantage of very significant reduction in brake block wear and hence time out of traffic, as well as providing a smoother braking effort.

The provision on a large scale of miniature circuit breakers eased fault finding, but whether the Design Panel's flattening of the cab front below the windows improved the appearance is a matter of opinion. One change which was definitely for the worse involved the adoption of axle-hung motors as compared to the bogie frame mounted motors driving through flexible couplings, which were employed on the earlier types. Experience of axle-hung motors on the diesel-electric Deltics operating at 100mph maximum speed had not had detrimental effects on the ECML, but the Co-Co wheel arrangement of the Deltics had permitted a 17½-ton axleload compared with the Class 86 Bo-Bo arrangement with 20½-ton axleload. The effect on the WCML track was disastrous and the excessively lively ride was not only uncomfortable when not downright alarming for crews but was even less tolerable on an electric locomotive than on a diesel because of the effects on current collection via the pantograph.

BR turned to the German Federal Railways for inspiration in solving the riding problems and adopted the Flexicoil secondary suspension involving nests of three helical springs supporting the body at each bogie side. Tests were carried out on No E3173 (late No 86204) in 1969 earning it the nickname 'Zebedee' after the Magic Roundabout TV programme character.

For the solution to the problems posed by the high unsprung mass of the axle hung

traction motors, BR turned to Sweden where Svenska Aktiebolaget Bromsregulator of Malmo had been successfully manufacturing resilient rubber cushioned wheels for a number of railway administrations. The SAB wheels were tried on No E3129 (later No 86205) as well as the Flexicoil testbed machine No E3173 in September 1971. During these trials the bogie frames on the class as a whole began to suffer fractures and, with the decision to extend electrification from Weaver Junction to Glasgow, the problems were overcome by fitting 49 locomotives with new bogies incorporating Flexicoil suspensions and SAB wheels and re-classified 86/2. The first three conversions (re-classified 86/1 in 1974) were fitted with new bogies with frame mounted traction motors and were intended as testbeds for the equipment to be carried by the new Class 87. The less ambitious modifications accorded to what are now Class 86/2 took place between mid 1973 and mid 1974 and, by the end of 1974, similar treatment for a further nine was authorised. The remaining locomotives, retaining their original bogies, were classified 86/0 and were restricted to 80mph maximum speed and thus were limited to freight working. In 1980, 19 Class 86/0 locomotives were fitted with resilient wheels but not Flexicoil suspension, becoming Class 86/3s. In 1984 a start was made in fitting all the Class 86/0s and 86/3s with Class 86/2 type bogies, their new classification, 86/4, reflecting the fact that they were equipped for multiple operation and had push-pull decoders. The Class 86/4s have AEI 282AZ traction motors with a continuous rating of 3,600hp at rail whereas the Class 86/2s have the 282BZ version rated at 4,400hp.

The Class 86/2 locomotive chosen for Anglia East work remain allocated to Willesden depot, where they return for Class 'E' examinations, being hauled dead over the North London line. From 1985 six locomotives were diagrammed to work all Liverpool Street–Norwich services as far as Ipswich, except for the last three down services and one summer Saturday extra to Yarmouth. They were also diagrammed for newspaper and mail services to Southend, but the lack of an electrified crossover at the Victoria terminal was perhaps the reason why their appearances proved to be the exception rather than the rule. The rosters called for up to four return trips to Ipswich per day involving 550 miles in revenue-earning service.

The May 1986 timetable saw a further three locomotives drafted to the GE, the Harwich Parkeston Quay service requiring an up and down daily boat train throughout the year plus an additional unadvertised service on certain days. One diagram involved the 03.20 Liverpool Street–Clacton newspaper service; when not required for the additional boat train, the locomotive was used

No 86 246 arriving at Manningtree with the 11.30 Liverpool Street–Norwich on 14 October 1985. The trees lining the track at this point combined with the curvature and gradient, made this a very difficult location for starting up services to London in the late autumn of 1986, which produced damper conditions at leaf fall time than the previous year.

Left: No 86 214 arriving at Manningtree South Junction, with its double-arm pantograph fully extended to clear the level crossing. The feeder station which necessitates the neutral section can been seen to the right of the train, the 09.30 Norwich–Liverpool Street, on 14 October 1985.

on the 11.12 Colchester–Liverpool Street parcels. Electric haulage of the Southend newspaper service was discontinued. The penultimate weekday Norwich service went over to electric locomotive haulage to obviate the need for an early morning empty coaching stock working which had featured in the previous year's diagrams.

From May 1987 the GE electric services called for 18 locomotives to operate 15 diagrams, which included the full Anglia West service as well as the extension of Anglia East to Norwich. The Parkeston Quay to Scotland 'European' service was diverted to run via London and went over to electric haulage, providing the first direct link between the GE and other electrified networks, although until 1988 a diesel pilot will be required between Stratford and Camden Road.

The announcement of approval for the wiring of the North London line was accompanied by authorisation for four new Class 87/2 locomotives. Though a development of the Class 87, the new locomotives will differ from the 14-year-old design by incorporating thyristor control, and will take advantage of developments in power electronics, microprocessor control and diagnostics and traction power control. Externally, the streamlined cab ends will present a much sleeker appearance, especially as connecting pipework is to be concealed behind

hinged panels. Designed for both passenger and freight work, their maximum speed of 110mph may mean that they will not in fact see much work over the speed restricted North London line. Enthusiasts would be advised not to hold their breath while awaiting their appearance on the GE!

Class 306

The 92 three-car units introduced in 1949 for the Shenfield electrification set standards for inner suburban London stock which were only achieved again in the 1970s.

Visually, the Shenfield stock presented a satisfying aspect with the body sides sloping out very gently from under the guttering before tapering inwards in a pleasing curve from below the windows. The use of a system of five marker lights below one of the cab windows obviated the need for clumsy train describer panels. Since all units ran with the Driving Motor Brake at the country end, it was not necessary to festoon both cabs with cables for multiple working. One might perhaps criticise the lowering of the roof profile to accommodate the pantograph

above the brake compartment and driving cab, which resulted in a somewhat squat front end appearance at that end, but in the light of some of the following designs, the Shenfield units were masterpieces of industrial design!

Perhaps their biggest advance was in the internal layout of the carriages. GE commuters had been used to standing. Indeed, it is said that when Gresley's 436-seat quint-art sets were introduced overcrowding was sometimes such as to bend the frames and prevent the doors opening! Now, for the first time, the coach layout was designed with the standing passengers in mind. The open saloon layout, with two pairs of sliding doors per car, allowed a nine-car Shenfield set to seat 528 compared with the 872 in two quint-art sets. However, the standing room for 660 in the electric units gave them greater total carrying capacity than the locomotive-hauled sets and standing in the modern train was probably only marginally more uncomfortable than sitting wedged six to a side in the steam train! The Birmingham Railway Wagon & Carriage Company was one of the contractors for the Shenfield sets, and it is probably not coincidental

that this company had been involved in building new District and Metropolitan Line stock of classes O, P and Q for London Transport in 1936, since there were many points of visual similarity between the main line and Underground units, both internally and externally.

With the conversion of the Liverpool Street–Shenfield section to ac, the stock was rebuilt in 1960, resulting in quite a marked transformation in its appearance. The new electrical equipment was housed in the intermediate trailer. The distinctive diamond photograph of the original design was replaced by a double arm pantograph located above the brake compartment in its new position in the intermediate trailer. The recessed roof of the former motor car was built up to the normal profile, though the outline of the old shape could still be discerned, giving the appearance of 'eyebrows' above the cab windows. The marker lights were dispensed with and a central route describer box was fitted. Seating capacity was reduced by eight. Converted units were tested on the Colchester–Clacton branch before having the ac equipment isolated so as to be able to continue in service until 'conversion day'.

Left: *Being in short supply, electric locomotives had not then been diagrammed for heavy freight work, but a morning newspaper train to Clacton is hauled by a Class 86 locomotive, which is then used on Colchester–Liverpool Street vans when not required for special boat train duty. No 86 235 is seen passing Marks Tey signalbox on this working on 3 September 1986.*

Above: *The first GE emus did not last long enough to see service under Anglia East catenary, but many of them passed through the territory on their way to scrap-yards. No 306058 heads a rake of withdrawn stock stabled in Ipswich Lower Yard in December 1983.*

The Shenfield electrification had included the Fenchurch Street–Bow Junction section, and though catenary was installed, in the event no passenger services were timetabled over this route, although a weekly empty coaching stock working was diagrammed in order to keep the overhead clean. Thus the Class 306s were not new visitors to Fenchurch Street when they appeared in the first week of February 1953, but this time they were carrying passengers from Southend diverted via the GE Shenfield route because of the effect of the disastrous East Coast floods on the LTS tracks. Extension of the electrification saw the Class 306 sphere of activity widen to embrace Chelmsford and Southend Central, but they rarely strayed onto the NE London lines. One unit was diagrammed to work out as far as Colchester on winter Sundays in the late 1970s, but being devoid of toilet facilities they were usually confined to their inner suburban role although their wide vestibules made them popular for Christmas mail specials over a wider area.

For such a long-lived type the class survived remarkably intact – apart from the loss of one unit through fire and one through collision damage – until the Class 315 arrived to replace them in 1981. The Railway Correspondence & Travel Society organised a farewell tour, and preparation for this involved one unit running to Chingford in October 1981. The tour itself encompassed runs over both the GE and LTS routes to Southend as well as a trip down the main line to Colchester. A few survived to fulfil their role as Southend parcels units at Christmas 1981. A measure of the respect in which Ilford depot (their home throughout their 32-year lives) held them may be seen in the preservation of unit No 017 at the depot, where it has been restored to the original green livery. The unit returned to service in November 1986 during a Network SouthEast Day sponsored by a railway publisher. A few other cars survive in departmental use at Ilford, acting as seat carriers and confined to the depot precincts. Though their demise pre-dated the Anglia East electrification, a number of withdrawn units passed through Ipswich on their way to scrap dealers.

Class 307

By the time the Shenfield electrification was extended to Southend Victoria and Chelmsford, BR had devised the basic standards for the next generation of emu stock. Since most of the orders would be for the Southern, that region's

Refurbished Class 307 unit No 104 makes a solo run down the Southminster branch during overhead line equipment tests on 23 March 1986, having previously worked down coupled with No 305510.

requirements took precedence. Thus the next class of GE electrics reverted from open saloons and sliding doors to compartments and open bays with slam doors. SR feeling seems to have been that such a layout was better suited to outer suburban work and permitted shorter boarding and alighting times at stations, although as far as is known the Shenfield sliding door stock had not presented problems in this respect. The compartment layout of the AM7 stock as it became known provided 362 seats in four cars, a considerable advance on the 176 seats of a three-car Shenfield unit. Underframes were to the new standard of 63ft 5in length and bodies of 9ft 3in overall width. The original formation was DTSO, MBS, TC and DTS with toilets provided in the first and third vehicles. This was the first time on BR dc units that the motor coach had not taken the leading position. The new formation was held to be less stressful to the track since the leading bogie in either direction of travel would be unmotored and hence lighter. In outline the stock was very similar to the Southern Region 2EPB and 2HAP units and the LMR Class 501 stock, although initially no train describer panels were carried and the marker light arrangement of the Shenfield stock was per-petuated. The units were carried on BR MkII bogies which, under the motor coach each carried two nose-suspended axle-hung GEC 174hp motors. Some units were used on Chelmsford services from June 1956 although route maps in the coaches only showed stations to Southend. Experimental work with the units included the fitting of No 22S with a Stone Faively pantograph and of No 05S with Gresley bogies in an effort to improve the unsatisfactory ride of the BR MkII bogie.

Conversion of the Southend and Chelmsford routes to ac in 1960/1 saw the complete withdrawal of the Class 307 units for conversion at Stratford works. Services were maintained using Class 302 units destined for use on the LTS section and Class 304 on loan from the LMR. Because the additional equipment necessary for dual voltage ac operation could not be accommodated under the motor coach, the brake compartment and pantograph were transferred thence to the DTS and the flattened section of the motor coach roof was built up to full height. The units were reformed so that the two vehicles carrying electrical equipment were next to one another to minimise cable work. Weight rose from 139.5 tons to 148 tons. Seating capacity was unchanged. A Southern Region type of route indicator was fitted between the cab windows, but laid out to carry the BR four-character description by showing the first two characters above the last two. Germanium rectifiers were fitted at first but were replaced by silicon from 1972.

In 1959 unit No 03S was used as a testbed for the structural alterations described above, although it continued to run with dc equipment. It also received another modification in the form of an in-line describer panel set into the cab roof, destination blinds being moved to a position between the cab windows, and level with the top of them. While this arrangement was adopted for the sloping end stock of Classes 304, 305 and 308 it was removed from unit No 03S when it received its new electrical equipment. The rebuilding of the class was a protracted business, the last modified unit not entering traffic until mid 1965.

Few emu types undergo two major reconstructions during their life-time, but such has been the experience of Class 307. A major refurbishment scheme involving Class 305, 307 and 308 was announced in 1979. Class 307 was the first to be treated. Work involved moving the first-class accommodation to the former DTSO, opening out all compartments and providing gangway connections between the vehicles. Fluorescent lighting in place of tungsten, and melamine panelling instead of wood provided a brighter interior. Public address equipment was installed. Externally, the most noticeable alteration was the removal of the train describer panel, rendered redundant by modern signalling techniques. This went some way to restoring the original appearance, although now only two white marker lights are carried instead of the four of the original design. Despite the poor riding of the MkII bogie, this feature was retained, though after successful trials on unit No 307111 with later B4 bogies reclaimed from redundant hauled vehicles it was decided to institute a programme to fit these bogies to all refurbished units, with heavy-duty B5 bogies being used under the motor coaches. No 307111 was involved not only in trials of the B4 bogies but was observed running in March 1983 with a large amount of test equipment inside the unit, and with cameras mounted on the roof to observe pantograph movement. Problems with pantograph sway and de-wiring had seen the class banned from the tight curves of the NE London lines in 1975. They are also forbidden to run over single line sections such as the Braintree branch and the line to St Botolph's, though they are used on the Southminster branch after No 307104 had led the way with trial runs in March 1986. Alone among the refurbished classes, the work on the Class 307s also involved the removal of their voltage changeover equipment. Thus their use away from their original stamping ground of the Southend Victoria line has become more and more restricted. They have yet to be recorded under Anglia East catenary, and with the imminent removal of 75mph units away from the main line north of Shenfield they seem destined to remain strangers to the main lines to Ipswich and Norwich.

On the sign:

DANGER
LIVE RAIL

Conductor rail charged with
electricity at 750volts is laid
alongside many of the sidings
in these works.

OU ARE WARNED THAT IT IS
NGEROUS TO STEP ON, TOUCH
COME IN CONTACT WITH THE
UCTOR RAIL OR ITS CONNECTIONS

Class 302

This type had the distinction of inaugurating the country's first 25kV ac passenger service between Colchester and Clacton in March 1969. Construction of the 112 four-car units ultimately destined for service on the former LTS route to Southend had been advanced in order that trial running could be carried out on the testbed provided by the Colchester–Clacton and Walton branches. The pioneering role of the new units also saw them employed for driver training purposes on the Styal line and on the Glasgow electrified routes.

While the units soon reached their intended destination of Southend, it was not via the LTS route to Central but by way of the GE line to Victoria, since conversion of the latter route to ac in November 1960 had seen only 30 Class 306 and Class 307 units similarly converted. When ac power reached Chelmsford in March 1961, Class 302 units performed a similar holding operation on that section of route. Class 302 units again came to the rescue following the traumas experienced on the North East London Class 305 units which had entered service in November 1960. Within three months, around 30 Class 302s were working NE London services, some reduced to three cars by the removal of their trailer composites to suit that line's operating conditions. Even with this assistance, dmu

The extensive refurbishment programme of GE emus announced in 1979 called for the combined resources of both Wolverton and Eastleigh Works. Class 302 unit No 251 is seen in SR third rail territory in October 1985 awaitig treatment.

replacements were necessary on some services. The Class 302s' 'white knight' image suffered a nasty shock however (no pun intended!) in November 1961 when it had been hoped to institute the full LTS electric service. Insulation trouble in the Class 302s' traction motors meant that a mixed steam and electric service was the best that could be provided until June 1962, by when the offending motors had been rewound. Thereafter the class settled down to a more humdrum existence, being principally confined to the LTS route, although some units work on the line which first gave them employment, the Colchester–Clacton branch. As a prelude to the refurbishment programme set No 210 received Class 312 type bogies for trial purposes in 1978.

Externally, the units bore an even closer resemblance to the SR 2EPB and 2HAP types than did the Class 307s, since the Class 302s were provided at the outset with train describer panels. Only the grouping of brake and multiple working connections and the omission of guttering strips above the cab windows on the GE type marked them apart. The original formation of the Class 302s

G.E. ELECTRIC MULTIPLE UNITS 1949–1987

Class (TOPS designation)	Date of introduction	No. of sets built	No. of cars per set	Weight of set (tons)	No. of motors per set	Continuous rating (hp)	No. of seats per set	Length of set (ft)	Acceleration rate (mph/sec)	Maximum speed (mph)	Rebuilt (RB) Refurbished (RF) date	Weight of set (tons)	No. of seats per set
306[1]	1949	92	3	104	4	185	176	170	1.25	75	RB 1960	105	168
307	1956	32	4	140	4	174	363	266	1.1	75	RB 1961	149	363
											RF 1981–2	155	326
302[2,7]	1958	112	4	155	4	192	363	266	1.1	75	RF 1985	163	326
305/1[2]	1959	52	3	123	4	205	266	200	1.35	75			
305/2[2]	1960	19	4	153	4	205	363	266	1.1	75	RF 1982	157	326
308/1[2]	1961	33	4	154	4	192	363	266	1.1	75	RF 1983–4	156	326
308/2[2,8]	1961	9	4	153	4	192	267	200	1.1	75			
308/3[2]	1962	3	3	119	4	192	272	200	1.35	75			
309/1[3]	1962	8	2	99	4	282	207	133	0.8	100	RF 1985–	170	228
309/2[4]	1962	8	4	168	4	282	172	266	0.8	100	RF 1985–	169	226
309/3	1962	7	4	167	4	282	212	266	0.8	100			
310[5]	1966	49	4	158	4	270	318	266	1.1	75	RF 1986–	161	314
308/4[2,9]	1971	4	4	154	4	192	343	266	1.1	75			
312/1[2]	1975	19	4	154	4	270	322	266	0.9	90			
313	1976	64	3	106	8	110	232	200	1.5	75			
312/0	1977	26	4	154	4	270	322	266	0.9	90			
315[6]	1980	61	4	128	8	110	318	266	1.4	75			

Notes: Data in the first eleven columns refers to the stock when first introduced. Significant variations on rebuilding (to a.c.), refurbishment or reformation of sets are detailed in the last three columns or in the notes.

[1] Dual voltage on rebuilding.
[2] Dual voltage (25kV/6.25kV).
[3] Received 2 additional trailers from 1973, becoming 309/4, then had one removed (309/5). Have now regained second trailer and are classified 309/1.
[4] Originally Griddle Car sets. Griddles removed 1981.
[5] Originally built for LMR. Transferred to GE 1987.
[6] 315/1 41 sets having British electrical equipment 315/0 20 sets with GEC equipment.
[7] 30 units refurbished 29 units received interim refurbishment 1982.
[8] MLV sets. Converted to 3 car 1984 (DTLV + MLV + BDTS) Acceleration rate 1.35 mph/sec.
[9] Converted from 308/2.

followed that of the Class 307 units before conversion; DTS, MBC, TC and DTC. The Class 302s rode on Gresley double-bolster bogies introduced in an effort to improve the ride experienced on the earlier Class 307s. The Class 302 units were included in the refurbishment scheme of 1979, which involved similar work to that on Class 307 units, including the removal of the train describer panels. In the event an interim refurbishment was afforded to 29 units in 1982 before a further 30 were accorded full refurbishment treatment in 1985. The remainder contain blue asbestos, and unless refurbished, will be withdrawn when replacements are available. Withdrawals commenced in 1983, although refurbished unit No 302263 was displayed to the West Midlands Passenger Transport Executive at Birmingham International in November 1984 as a possible replacement for Class 304. Refurbishment has reduced seating capacity from 363 to 326.

The final unit of the class was used for experimental purposes when first built, emerging with silicon rectifier and Brentford transformer. This was replaced in 1964 by thyristor control equipment, the first application of this type in the country. Presumably in the interests of standardisation, this was removed in 1972 after experience of this important new development in traction control had been gained.

Several re-formations of units have taken place, of which the strangest was that which occurred when unit No 244 lost a driving trailer in a mishap. Its replacement was from a Class 504 Bury line 1,200V dc unit which had been in store. Though suitably rebuilt with respect to its driving equipment, it nevertheless retained its sloping cab end. Subsequent withdrawal of set No 250 released one of its trailers for its sister unit, which thus regained its symmetrical looks.

It was a pair of Class 302 units which made up the first timetabled public electric service to Ipswich, when Nos 243 and 266 formed the 10.30 from Liverpool Street as far as Ipswich on 18 April 1985, as the usual locomotive-hauled stock had suffered a failure. Subsequent appearances of the type in the Anglia East area have been rare, although No 302219 was paired with No 308135 on the 14.12 stopping service from Ipswich on 30 September 1985, and No 302205 was formed with Nos 308139 and 308145 on a relief service from Colchester to Ipswich during the evening of 28 April 1986.

Class 305

As already mentioned, the Class 305 units built for the North East London electrification got off to a disastrous start. While contemporary criticism focused blame on the adoption of the dual 25kV/ 6.25kV ac system, it overlooked the fact that Class 302 units coped satisfactorily with voltage changeovers. The distinguishing feature of the Class 305s, and the villain of the piece, was the Com-Pak GEC rectifier originally fitted. This was also used in the Class 84 electric locomotives, but did not have to cope with voltage changeover in that environment. The Com-Pak rectifier was of an excitron type as opposed to the ignitron used on Class 302 units. At this early stage of ac traction work, power units relied on tanks of mercury acting as a cathode in the process of rectifying ac current from the overhead to dc for the traction motors. Single-anode rectifiers were preferred, since they were easier to replace in the case of failure than multi-anode types. But with a single-anode rectifier the flow of electrons is extinguished when the anode goes into the negative half cycle of the ac current and the mercury arc is suppressed. In the ignitron, the arc was re-struck at the start of the positive half cycle, making the rectifier less likely to conduct in the reverse direction, and so permitted the anode and the cathode to be closer together, saving space and giving a lower voltage drop across the rectifier because of the shorter arc. On the other hand the excitron deflected the arc to an auxiliary anode during the negative half cycles, so avoiding the complications of re-striking the arc. The Com-Pak rectifier aimed to capitalise on this aspect, while combining the low voltage drop and compact size of the ignitron.

The problems encountered on the NE London and contemporary Glasgow dual voltage electrifications were serious enough to warrant the fitting-out of one Class 305 train as a mobile laboratory to assist the Chief Inspecting Officer of Railways to compile his report. The most serious failures on the Class 305 units were identified as breakdowns in traction motors and battery chargers, while the rectifier suffered intermittent failure due to current loss associated with pantograph bounce. The traction motors also proved vulnerable to the rapid action of the circuit breaker as the train passed through neutral sections which were relatively closely spaced on the NE London lines. The units were withdrawn for modification by GEC, the major work entailing the substitution of the mercury arc rectifiers by silicon semi-conductor rectifiers of the type which had been fitted experimentally in the final Class 305 unit when built.

The start of ac unit construction with Class 302s had seen a switch away from the SR as builder of GE units, subsequent work taking place at York and Doncaster. While Class 302 units had followed traditional SR outlines, the Class 305 benefitted from improvements inspired by the Design Panel in the shape of a somewhat less undistinguished front end, where the top half of the cab sloped backwards and the train describer panel was incorporated in the cab roof. The same style was adopted on the later Class 308 units for the GE as well as the Class 304 units of the LMR.

Fifty-two 3-car units of Class 305/1 were built for the Chingford and Enfield services; nineteen four-car units formed Class 305/2 for services to Bishop's Stortford and Hertford East. In the three-car sets the seating is entirely in second class open saloons and a single large window is fitted between the doors to the seating bays. The four-car sets originally provided first-class seating in a trailer composite and have pairs of windows between the doors. Aesthetically, the design is not helped by the fact that tops of the door droplights are at a lower height than the fixed window tops. All units have toilets. The motor brake seconds of both types have four 205hp motors. On the three-car sets this provides an acceleration rate of 1.35mph/sec while the slightly lower 1.10mph/sec rate of the four-car sets is deemed adequate for their outer suburban work. Gresley bogies are fitted to both types.

1983 brought upheaval to the ordered ranks of the Class 305/1 and Class 305/2 units. Class 305/2s were going to Wolverton for refurbishment and Clapton tunnels were closed for work involved in raising the line voltage to 25kV. A batch of 17 Class 305/1 units was withdrawn as a step towards the elimination of stock with blue asbestos content. Six more received trailers from Class 308/2 and Class 308/4 units, causing them to be reclassified initially as 305/3. These conversions were short-lived, however, being withdrawn by the year's end save for their trailer composites, two of which were formed into surviving Class 305/1s to provide four-car units for shuttle work in connection with the closure of Clapton tunnels. To add to the confusion, Class 305/2 units were sometimes to be seen operating as three-car sets. Even more oddly, two Class 308 units were briefly renumbered into the 305 series, probably in error. The situation finally resolved itself with the decision to facelift the Class 305/1s as opposed to providing the full refurbishment afforded their four-car sisters.

The 'Jazz Train' stickers applied to the cab fronts of the Class 305/1s in October 1983 to mark the GLC-sponsored augmentation of NE London services proclaim that they will remain on these services, assisted by the newer Class 315s. The Class 305/2s may gravitate to LTS services when sufficient Class 310 units from the LMR arrive to release them from the Bishop's Stortford (and from January 1987) Cambridge services.

In March 1985, units No 506 and 517 were observed with the names *River Lea* and *River Stort* respectively on their cab sides. Naming of emu stock had previously been confined to the Brighton Belle and the APT sets, and the powers-that-be obviously considered that the Class 305s were suffering from delusions of grandeur since the names were soon removed.

Some Class 305/1 units have ended up in departmental service. No 435 has served as a mobile classroom ahead of electrification schemes and appeared at Ipswich and Cambridge in this capacity while unit No 438 was taken into departmental stock at Crewe and ran special push-pull tests between Crewe and Wolverhampton with locomotive No 87 101 in March 1986.

Perhaps it is appropriate that Class 305 units formed the first electric train to work into Suffolk under its 'own' power, since as long ago as August 1978 unit No 412 was recorded at Liverpool Street displaying 'Ipswich' on its destination blinds! The type was also employed on similar overhead line equipment tests when 305510 participated in the Southminster branch trials in March 1986. Unit No 451 took part in the Romford–Upminster tests the following month. While Class 305 sets remain on the latter branch, the type has yet to reappear elsewhere in Anglia East territory.

Class 308

With the spread of ac working down the GE main line to Chelmsford and Colchester linking up with the Clacton/Walton lines in the early 1960s, further orders were placed for emu stock. Externally identical to the Class 305/2 units, the 33 four-car sets of Class 308/1 differed only in being fitted with English Electric as opposed to AEI electrical equipment. The three Class 308/3 units delivered a year later in 1962 omitted the trailer composite of the Class 308/1s, making them virtually the same as the three-car Class 305/1 units. This similarity was to lead to an identity crisis in later life when one unit, No 454, was to be seen carrying the class prefix 305 on one driving car and 308 on the other, while No 453 was at least consistently wrong in carrying 305 on both ends!

The nine units of Class 308/2 saw an innovation for emu stock since these four-car units, destined for LTS use, incorporated a motor luggage van in place of the MBS of the main sub-class. Although subsequently used for parcels, mails and news-papers, these trains were originally intended for Hapag Lloyd boat train services to Tilbury, which had been transferred from St Pancras to Fenchurch Street. The SR had adopted the principle of separate self-propelled luggage vans in 1959, extending the multiple-unit concept by adopting a scheme dating back to the GWR parcels railcar of the late 1930s and emulated in the BR dmu fleet. While such cars obviously offered greater operating flexibility they required their own traction motors and two sets of driving equipment. The Class 308/2 arrangement was clearly cheaper, but in the light of the fleet's subsequent history it might have been better to have followed the SR lead. As traffic intensified on the LTS it was no longer practical to confine the Class 308/2s to boat train and off-peak services, and the loss of 96 seats when they were used on rush-hour trains did not endear them to commuters. Four units had the MLVs rebuilt as MBSOs at Wolverton in 1971, becoming Class 308/4 in the process. The remaining five Class 308/2s continued unaltered until 1983 when their TC cars were removed and they were renumbered 991-5. The following year Nos 992 5 were rebuilt to fit their more specialised role in the Parcels Sector, when one DTS was converted into a parcels van. Unit No 991 was fitted with an observation window in one driving trailer in order that pantograph movements could be observed, before it ultimately retired into departmental stock for use as a breakdown train. No 992 was withdrawn. While the Class 308/3 and Class 308/4 units were withdrawn in 1985, the Class 308/1s received refurbishment treatment and are destined for use on the LTS section together with the Class 305/2 units.

The Class 308/1s have participated in Anglia East services from the first, being utilised on early morning up stopping services from Ipswich as well as having a midday working for a brief spell. Unit No 991 was employed in testing the overhead line equipment on the Upminster branch in April 1986. Class 308 Nos 140 and 150 formed the first electric train to traverse the Harwich branch when used in similar tests in the same month.

Class 309

The completion of the catenary linking Liverpool Street to Clacton in 1962 gave BR the opportunity to develop a new concept in ac design, the express multiple-unit. It was a chance they almost did not take, since the unfortunate experiences with dual-voltage emus on the NE London electrification led to the consideration of electric locomotive haulage for the Clacton expresses. Steadier nerves prevailed, and the first Class AM9 units entered revenue-earning service in January 1963. Seen at the time as the forerunners of a fleet of high-speed emus, the Class 309s remained the only units with 100mph capability until the advent of the Advanced Passenger Train. Although at first the maximum speed could not be utilised due to speed restrictions, the Commonwealth bogies on which the units were mounted gave a very smooth ride and continued to do so many years later when track improvements permitted the designed speed to be attained. Some SR main line emu stock had been partially fitted with Commonwealth bogies but the Class AM9 units saw its first complete application to emu stock. After comparative trials of pre-nationalisation coach types

between Marylebone and Nottingham, BR had developed a standard bogie based largely on a GWR design, but this suffered from excessive wear after relatively low mileages. As an interim measure the US Commonwealth bogie, a much sturdier structure with coil spring secondary suspension, was adopted while BR finalised design work on its own B4 bogies.

Visually, the pleasing effect of the wrap-round cab windows so successfully introduced on the Glasgow 'Blue Trains' was spoiled on the Clacton units by the operating requirement for gangway connections between units, which also necessitated sets of air pipes either side to ease coupling procedures. The practice of splitting and joining Walton branch trains at Thorpe-le-Soken meant that through connections were needed to give all passengers access to the griddle cars, which were carried in eight of the 15 four-car units. Eight two-car units were also provided. All sets were equipped with four 282hp motors, the idea being that two-car sets could be added to stopping trains at peak periods so that the enhanced power/weight ratio would boost acceleration away from stations. Such a 4+4+2 combination boasted a power/weight ratio of 7.79hp/ton compared to the 6.76hp/ton of the almost contemporary 4CIG units on the SR. The Clacton units' acceleration rate of 0.8mph/sec was not as high as that of suburban stock, but the Class AM9s were designed to maintain it into the higher ranges of speed.

The distinctiveness of the Class AM9s was reinforced by their original livery of maroon. Double glazing was another feature introduced on the class, but this was removed within a couple of years because of the difficulty experienced in maintaining the vacuum between the panes, needed to prevent condensation. This was but the start of a gradual decline in the refinements of the class, which was not to be arrested until the advent of Anglia East. The next indignity was the replacement of the wrap-round windscreens by two flat panes and a corner pillar, since the wrap-round design was costly to replace when broken. Next the griddle cars lost their movable armchairs and ceased to serve hot food in 1971 before being withdrawn completely and replaced by former locomotive-hauled trailer seconds in 1981. The 309/2 sub classification of the griddle sets thus ceased to have significance, and they were merged with the Class 309/3 four-car units. The two-car sets had been classified 309/1 but four of them were strengthened to four cars by the addition of former locomotive-hauled MkI vehicles,

Overleaf: *Shorn of its third rail pick-up gear, Class 313 unit No 037 sits alongside native emus at Colchester on 13 March 1981. Four of these units spent a spell based at Clacton from 1981 to 1983.*

Refurbished Class 310 unit No 084, resplendent in Network SouthEast livery passes Marks Tey during braking tests between Witham and Colchester which were run during the first week of September 1986. These 75mph units seem likely to be confined to Cambridge and Southend Victoria services when they are transferred from the LMR. It seems likely that the GE will have to wait until 1995 before receiving new units in the shape of the revolutionary 'Networker' sets with ac traction motors.

becoming Class 309/4 in 1973/4. Similar treatment befell the remaining Class 309/1 units in 1980/1 before all Class 309/4s had one vehicle removed to make them Class 309/5s!

In the midst of these re-formations an odd intruder infiltrated the GE emu fleet in the shape of dmu buffet car from a Swindon Inter City unit which was drafted into unit No 616 in 1972 to replace its accident damaged griddle car. It was distinguished by its B4 bogies until withdrawn along with the other griddle cars in 1981.

By the nature of their role as express units, the Class 309 sets were confined to the Clacton services until the Anglia East extensions enabled them to go further afield. Their high speed capability saw them involved in several tests on the WCML. The tests in 1970 presaged the introduction of HST services and Class 309 units were used together with No E3173 (later No 86204) and Deltic No D9020. The trials were between Tring and Leighton Buzzard and part of the tests involved the use of dummy passengers on Cheddington station in order to determine safe distances from the platform edge when high speed services were passing. In 1976 unit No 604 ran high-speed trials on the West Coast Main Line to test new equipment. In June 1983 a 309 ran trials on the Braintree branch, and November 1986 saw another return to the WCML this time in passenger service in the form of an enthusiasts' special from Euston to Manchester.

Despite the fact that the units had all amassed mileages in excess of four million by 1984, their excellent reliability record (the Monopolies & Mergers Commission Report on London and Southeast services identified the Class 309s as top of the reliability league with just 0.35 casualties per 100,000 miles) and the requirements of the Anglia East programme saw the announcement of a £17.5 million refurbishment programme for the class. All will become four-car units, and to this end the Class 309/5s will gain an extra locomotive-hauled coach, becoming Class 309/1s and differing from the original four-car units of Class 309/2 mainly in that their motor equipment is in a driving coach, whereas in the latter sub-class it is in an intermediate MBS.

Somewhat ironically almost as the original griddle cars were finally broken-up, Travellers Fare reinstated catering facilities on the Class 309s in September 1984, albeit on a more modest scale by taking over one compartment for the sale of light refreshments.

The first refurbished unit, No 605, resplendent in the new London and South East Sector livery of two-tone brown and orange was used on a press run to Ipswich on 17 April 1985, becoming the first passenger-carrying electric service to Suffolk. The return run was announced to the public as an additional service and thus became the first revenue-earning electric train from Ipswich. When the electric services timetable came into force the following month Class 309s were diagrammed for two down semi-fasts to Ipswich during the evening peak, the latter being extended to Stowmarket from August 1985 after a pair of Class 309 units had been used to test the overhead line equipment between Ipswich and Stowmarket on 20 June. The Stowmarket train returns empty to Ipswich where it waits to form the last up service. The earlier train returns empty from Ipswich. The energising of the Harwich branch saw the Class 309s taking on the role of boat train in the shape of the twice daily Essex Continental, the first services proudly carrying headboards. The class had had an unusual rehearsal for this part the previous year when on certain summer Saturday shortage of stock had necessitated their use on relief boat trains from Parkeston, hauled between Colchester and Harwich by a Class 37 diesel. In the up direction, permission was granted for the electric units to raise their pantographs once energised overhead had been regained past Manningtree in order to charge their air brake system and permit a shorter stop at Colchester where the diesel locomotive was detached.

Further evidence of the reviving fortunes of Class 309 came in 1985 when refurbished units began to carry telephone facilities. They now provide Anglia East with semi-fast services second to none.

Class 310

As has already been seen, from the late 1960s the GE slipped down the priority list when it came to the allocation of new stock and has had to make do with refurbishing its own units or receiving equipment cascaded from other routes. With the refurbishment programme in full swing in 1984 it was time to take stock of the situation. The approval of the ECML electrification was seen as an opportunity to ease the capacity constraints over the two-track Welwyn bottleneck imposed by the running of 90mph Class 312/0s between 125mph HSTs by ordering 20 new Class 317/2 units with 100mph capacity. The GN Class 312s would thus be released for transfer to the GE, where they would enable all workings on the main line north of Shenfield to be entrusted to units with 90mph top speed, so maximising the capacity of the line thence to Colchester, which forms BR's most intensively used stretch of double track.

With the announcement of approval for the Snow Hill electrification linking the Midland line from Bedford to the SR network, new dual-voltage Class 319 units were ordered which will render the native Class 317/1 redundant. These will move to the southern end of the WCML, replacing Class 310 units which will be refurbished for services on the

Cambridge line and later to Stansted Airport. To this end, Class 310 unit No 084 ran braking trials between Witham and Colchester during the first week of September 1986.

When introduced in 1965, the Class 310s set new standards in emu appearance, breaking away decisively from the MkI carriage look with a load-bearing integrally constructed body which dispensed with the underframe, thus giving sufficient room for all electrical equipment to be accommodated below floor height, so allowing the simplification of cooling by natural airflow. The oil radiator and fan used on earlier emus could thus be dispensed with, reducing maintenance and noise levels. Compared to a four-car Class 309 set, weight was reduced from 172 tons to 158 tons. The B4 bogies of the Class 310s were equipped with disc brakes, in their first large-scale application on BR.

The front end design seemed to combine the best aspects of the Class 305, 308 and 309 cabs, having the slightly raked-back upper half and roof-mounted train describer of the former, and the wrap-round windscreens of the Clacton units but without the excrescence of the gangway connection. As on the Class 309 units these stylish screens were subsequently replaced by flat panes.

Perhaps because most of their original operating area was over four track lines, a maximum speed of 75mph was deemed adequate.

Class 312

The success of the Class 310s was borne out by the decision virtually to replicate the design ten years later in 1975. For the first time in ac unit design, a common type was produced for service on three different sections. The GE received its first new units for 13 years in the shape of 19 Class 312/1s, their classification indicating that they were dual-voltage units. Four Class 312/2 units for the LMR lines around Birmingham followed in 1976. These were restricted to the 75mph maximum speed of their Class 310 cousins, while 1977 saw a further 26, classified 312/0, for service on the GN suburban electrified routes.

The number of diodes in the rectifier was reduced from 48 to 16 compared with Class 310 and this, combined with advances in constructional techniques, saw weight reduced from 158 tons to 151 tons. Externally the units were very similar to Class 310, although flat windscreens were provided from new and the recesses for multiple working

The old order on the Harwich branch. A two-car Metro-Cammell dmu provides one of the 15 daily all-stations shuttles between Manningtree and Harwich Town current in the 1985 timetable. From May 1986, 15 electric trains continued to call at all five stations giving a 21-minute service for the 11¼ miles, just two minutes faster than the dmus, though three of the electric services provided through facilities to Liverpool Street for the intermediate stations.

connections reached almost to the bottom of the cab windows. (What a pity that these unsightly appendages could not have been hidden behind sliding or removable panels.) The Class 312 units employed BT8 bogies under the non powered cars and BP14 bogies under the motor coach. They were gangwayed throughout, unlike the Class 310 units in which initially the intermediate coaches were not connected. Public address facilities were fitted.

The Class 312/1 units were mainly confined to Clacton line services until 1985 when they were also used to provide most of the two-hourly stopping services to Ipswich. Class 312s provided the first electric passenger service from Stowmarket from 8 August 1985 and began working to Harwich from May 1986. The delivery of Class 317/2 units to Hornsey for use on the GN in 1986 enabled the transfer of Class 312/0 units to the GE to begin in May, their single voltage capacity no longer a bar to operation over most of the GE. When sufficient Class 317 units are cascaded onto the LMR, the four Class 312/2 units will move to the GE. Unless they are re-geared for higher speed they are unlikely to penetrate Anglia East territory, since by the time they arrive there should be sufficient 90mph Class 312s to oust 75mph units from the main line.

Class 313

The Class 313 units were the first production version of a new generation of suburban emus developed from the three PEP prototypes produced for the SR in 1971. Many of the prototype features were perpetuated in the production design; from the passengers' viewpoint the most significant was the power-operated sliding doors and open saloon layout. Although the principle used on the prototypes of powering each wheelset was not perpetuated on the Class 313s, each of the axles under both motor cars in the three car sets was powered. Current collection is via a pantograph mounted on the intermediate unpowered trailer, which houses the underfloor rectifier equipment and via shoe beams on the motor cars; since these sets were designed for inner suburban work on the GN electric services involving running over third rail 750V dc between Drayton Park and Moorgate, making this the first dual system stock on BR.

The resistances in the Class 313 units are used for rheostatic braking and heat is recovered from them for use in the motor coaches. The BX1 bogies

With the cascading of Class 312 units from the GN, it is hoped to divert the 75mph types away from services on the main line north of Shenfield, which as far as Colchester forms BR's most intensively used double-track route. Native GE unit No 312787 is paired with ex GN No 717 on a Colchester service entering Chelmsford on 15 November 1986.

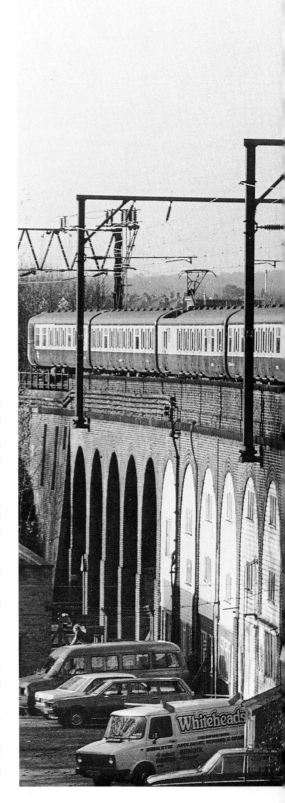

incorporate air spring secondary suspension. Pressure on these springs is measured automatically and used to control the current flow so as to maintain the very nippy rate of acceleration of 1.5mph/sec in all states of loading.

Visually the sloping cab ends of the PEP prototype was not adopted, but the imaginative wrap-round effect of the yellow front end gave a pleasing appearance enhanced by the absence of the profusion of multiple working pipes which had detracted from the appearance of earlier units. These connections were incorporated in the American 'Tightlok' coupler. The interconnecting doors were neatly recessed and, being provided for staff and emergency use only, dispensed with the corridor connections, to present a very clean and neat appearance.

Unfortunately reliability was initially very poor with failures occurring on average once every 7,600 miles, mainly due to problems with the sliding doors, and the tripcock mechanisms used on the Underground system. The 'Tightlok' couplers would only work on straight track and consequently units were not uncoupled off peak.

The type paid sporadic visits to the GE from an early date, two being used for test runs between Shenfield and Chelmsford and Southend Victoria in June 1979. One was subsequently displayed at the Stratford depot Open Day the following month.

In 1981 four units had their third rail shoe gear removed, and they were used on the Clacton branch until late 1983. Some units were then required to provide relief on the 'Bed-Pan' line, whose new Driver-Only Operation (DOO) Class 317s had not benefitted from a year lying idle due to an industrial dispute. June 1986 saw Class 313s replacing Class 501 units on the Watford dc services, and brought them back to the GE, this time in their dual-voltage mode on Watford–Liverpool Street trains over the new Graham Road curve. The type returned to Clacton branch service in late autumn 1986.

Class 315

Built in 1980–1, Class 315 was a four-car derivative of Class 313, the main difference being the adoption of thyristor control, first seen in a production version on the three-car Class 314s for the Clyde Rail electric services, although a derivative of the type first used experimentally on a Class 302 unit back in 1964. Like the Scottish units, dual sourcing was used for the traction motors, 41 of the GE units having Brush motors while GEC supplied 20 sets. The last three units delivered dispensed with the small train describer panel above one cab window and this was subsequently blanked out on earlier units.

Before delivery to the GE, two units were loaned to the LMR for driver training on the 'Bed-Pan'

electric lines and indeed it was a Class 315 unit which unexpectedly inaugurated electric passenger services, when it was pressed into traffic between Bedford and Luton on 16 September 1981 to cover for a failed diesel train.

On the GE, driver training trips took them to Colchester and Southend Victoria, and once in service they began to extend their sphere of activity to Southend Victoria before complaints about their lack of toilet facilities saw them restricted to the inner suburban diagrams of the Shenfield stock which they had replaced. Unlike the Class 306 units, they began to venture onto the NE London lines from January 1984. Their single voltage capacity was no longer a bar to operation on these routes, since the final section between Clapton and Cheshunt had been converted to 25kV in 1983.

With the units now working beyond the confines of the slow lines to Shenfield they are more likely to run between services composed of other types, although in the event of failure the 'Tightlok' couplers present difficulties when coming to the assistance of (or being assisted by) units of other classes. Couplers are being modified to overcome this problem, and units so treated carry a white sticker above their number. Unit No 813 was fitted with a tachograph device, resulting in its being 'blacked' by drivers.

Although the type seems unlikely to penetrate Anglia East territory in service, one unit has travelled the main line to Norwich when it was towed north to the Crown Point Open Day in September 1983.

Liveries

Since livery details were largely common to all the emu types they may conveniently be described at one point. All units built before 1966 except the Clacton stock originally carried green livery. When new, the Class 309s wore maroon, attractively offset by a central lining stripe on the bodyside — something which would have helped relieve the rather unimaginative treatment of the other stock. From 1966, all the existing GE emu stock, again excepting the Class 309s, began to appear in blue livery, the Clactons receiving the more distinguished blue and grey reserved for main line stock. From

Newly painted Class 312 unit No 708 brings yet another livery variation to GE lines, the grey, red, white and blue of Network SouthEast. Since electrification work started, the old corporate identity blue-and-grey has yielded to new colours for Inter-City on coaches, some Class 86/2s and one Stratford based Class 47, the Essex Express livery for refurbished Class 309s, large logo treatment for passenger diesels and Railfreight livery for freight machines as well as the latest innovation, the Network SouthEast colours. NSE territory ends at Manningtree, and diagramming requirements mean that new liveried stock is often to be found on inappropriate duties.

Belstead Bank – 1: *No 37 109 hammers up the 1 in 120/130 bank soon after leaving Ipswich with the 07.19 Lowestoft–Liverpool Street on 26 April 1984. Through working from Lowestoft ceased at the end of the 1983/4 timetable, due to the imminent resignalling of the East Suffolk line with radio electronic tokenless block.*

Belstead Bank – 2: *No 86 246* East Anglian Regiment *sails up the Bank and presents the pleasing, though still rare, sight of a complete train in the new Inter-City livery. Due to a speed restriction at the botton of the Bank, trains now ascend the once formidable incline faster than they descend.*

Overleaf *No 305450 and 308991 were used for tests on the Upminster branch on 13 April 1986. The ensemble is seen leaving Romford to return to Ilford after the tests. The picture as taken from the old Midland Railway section of the station which was burned down later in the year.*

1980, blue and grey was bestowed on all GE emus except Class 306 units whose lives were drawing to an end. Class 313 and 315 wore blue and grey from the outset.

The foregoing properly relates to the bodysides of the units only from 1960, for it was in that year that experiments began to improve the visibility of the railways' fast but quiet motive power. Units of classes 305, 306 and 307 at least are known to have appeared with a vertical yellow stripe running from the cab roof, between the windows, to the buffer beam. This somewhat bizarre arrangement soon gave way from about 1962 to rectangular yellow panels covering the full width of the cab front below the multiple working connections. By 1967 this had given way to full yellow front ends. It is known that on Classes 307 at least the yellow was at first continued back around the cabside windows, presaging the treatment given to the later Classes 313 and 315. The Class 309 units were dealt with in a similar manner and retained this feature which had been short-lived on Class 307s.

By 1982, the sectorisation of BR had spelled the end of the 'Corporate Identity'. The London and South East sector used the opportunity of the refurbishment of the Clacton stock to devise a very attractive new livery of two-tone brown separated by an orange stripe, leading to the soubriquet 'Jaffa Cake' among the enthusiast fraternity! The transfer of Chris Green from Scot Rail to become director of LSE resulted not only in the adoption of the Network

SouthEast brand name but also of a new livery of powder blue with red, white and grey stripes ending in airline-style chevrons. Units of types 309, 312 and 315 have received this livery to date, the sight of a Clacton train on October 1986 composed of one unit in old style blue and grey, one in 'Jaffa Cake' livery and one in Network stripes driving home the fact that the corporate identity has been laid to rest with a vengeance!

The future

By the summer of 1986, the 323 emus in GE service had an average age of just over 22 years, although this disguises the fact that many of the older types have been or are in the process of being refurbished. Classes 302, 305 and 308 retain dual voltage equipment still required for working on the LTS route.

As cascaded stock is received, one may expect the demise of the unrefurbished examples of Classes 302 and 305/1 as they contain blue asbestos. While both Anglia East and Anglia West have relied on more intensive working of existing emu stock, the opening of the Stansted Airport branch is expected to see five more refurbished Class 310s from the LMR and five new trains of Class 317 type stock. It will be interesting to see whether the opening of the North London ac overhead electrification will result in any interworking of electric units from the GN or LMR Lines, although none is planned at present.

Bibliography

AC Electric Locomotives of British Rail. Brian Webb and John Duncan. David & Charles, 1979.
British Electric Trains in Camera. John Glover. Ian Allan, 1982.
British Railways Engineering 1948–80. J. Johnson and R. A. Long. Mechanical Engineering Publications, 1981.
The Eastern since 1948. G. Freeman Allen. Ian Allan, 1981.
Electric Trains in Britain. B. K. Cooper. Ian Allan, 1979.
EMU & Electric Loco Profiles. British Rail, 1986.
The Great Eastern Railway. Cecil J. Allen. Ian Allan, 1975.

Modern Railways Insight – BR Electrification. Brian Perren, Ian Allan, 1986.
A Regional History of the Railways of Great Britain – The Eastern Counties. D. I. Gordon. David & Charles, 1968.
100 Years of Electric Traction. Colin J. Marsden. Oxford Publishing Company, 1985.

Periodicals

Ipswich Transport Society Bulletin
Modern Railways
The Railway Magazine
The Railway Observer
Trains Illustrated